Cambridge Elements

Elements in England in the Early Medieval World
edited by
Megan Cavell
University of Birmingham
Rory Naismith
University of Cambridge
Winfried Rudolf
University of Göttingen
Emily V. Thornbury
Yale University

NATURAL AND SUPERNATURAL IN EARLY MEDIEVAL ENGLAND

Richard Sowerby
University of Edinburgh

Shaftesbury Road, Cambridge CB2 8EA, United Kingdom

One Liberty Plaza, 20th Floor, New York, NY 10006, USA

477 Williamstown Road, Port Melbourne, VIC 3207, Australia

314–321, 3rd Floor, Plot 3, Splendor Forum, Jasola District Centre, New Delhi – 110025, India

103 Penang Road, #05–06/07, Visioncrest Commercial, Singapore 238467

Cambridge University Press is part of Cambridge University Press & Assessment, a department of the University of Cambridge.

We share the University's mission to contribute to society through the pursuit of education, learning and research at the highest international levels of excellence.

www.cambridge.org
Information on this title: www.cambridge.org/9781009619127

DOI: 10.1017/9781009175456

© Richard Sowerby 2025

This publication is in copyright. Subject to statutory exception and to the provisions of relevant collective licensing agreements, no reproduction of any part may take place without the written permission of Cambridge University Press & Assessment.

When citing this work, please include a reference to the DOI 10.1017/9781009175456

First published 2025

A catalogue record for this publication is available from the British Library

ISBN 978-1-009-61912-7 Hardback
ISBN 978-1-009-17544-9 Paperback
ISSN 2632-203X (online)
ISSN 2632-2021 (print)

Cambridge University Press & Assessment has no responsibility for the persistence or accuracy of URLs for external or third-party internet websites referred to in this publication and does not guarantee that any content on such websites is, or will remain, accurate or appropriate.

For EU product safety concerns, contact us at Calle de José Abascal, 56, 1°, 28003 Madrid, Spain, or email eugpsr@cambridge.org

Natural and Supernatural in Early Medieval England

Elements in England in the Early Medieval World

DOI: 10.1017/9781009175456
First published online: April 2025

Richard Sowerby
University of Edinburgh
Author for correspondence: Richard Sowerby, Richard.Sowerby@ed.ac.uk

Abstract: When men and women in early medieval England thought about the world around them, they did so in ways that often strike us as strange. Their surviving writings abound with unfamiliar ideas – about the creatures and beings which populated the world, about the forces and phenomena which shaped it, and about the ways in which human beings might enact change upon it through ritual, magic, and prayer. Although unfamiliar, these ideas provide important indications of how early medieval English thinkers characterized and categorized their surroundings and their experiences. Of substantial interest to many of them was the question of how they might distinguish correctly between what was 'natural' in the world, and what was not. This Element examines what that distinction meant to the inhabitants of early medieval England, and under what circumstances they felt compelled to explore it.

Keywords: early medieval, supernatural, nature, religion, magic

© Richard Sowerby 2025

ISBNs: 9781009619127 (HB), 9781009175449 (PB), 9781009175456 (OC)
ISSNs: 2632-203X (online), 2632-2021 (print)

Contents

Introduction	1
1 Creatures and Beings	5
2 Properties and Processes	22
3 Acts and Expectations	39
Final Thoughts	56
Bibliography	60

Natural and Supernatural in Early Medieval England 1

Introduction

When the Old English homilist Ælfric of Eynsham (d. c. 1010) spoke to people about the moon, he sometimes became defensive. There were, he understood, many people who believed that the moon exerted a mysterious influence upon human fortunes, and who believed that it was either lucky or unlucky to undertake particular activities on certain days in the lunar cycle. Beliefs of this kind were, in Ælfric's view, at best to be taken as a sign of stupidity, and quite possibly also as some form of 'heathen custom' that true Christians ought not to entertain.[1] At the same time, however, Ælfric had it on good authority from respected scholars that the moon really did hold great power over many things that happened in the world. The sea moved as one with it. Animals gained vigour and strength as it waxed above them, then weakened again as it waned. Trees which had been felled under the full moon provided wood which was harder and more durable than the timber which they might produce on any other day. All this had been established by observation and experience centuries ago, and Ælfric felt sure that *these* ideas about the moon did indeed deserve continued trust.[2] In a sermon composed for the first day of January – a day which Ælfric understood to be a major focus for all sorts of improper customs and beliefs – he felt compelled to justify to his congregation how it was that some claims about the power of the moon could be credited, while others could not. He explained that it was perfectly reasonable for him to believe that the moon influenced tidal motions, physical bodies, and the growth of trees, because 'this is no sorcery, but a natural thing through Creation' (*Nis þis nan wiglung ac is gecyndelic þing þurh gesceapenysse*).[3]

Ælfric's undeveloped remark indicates his willingness to accept that his world contained within it not only those things that were 'natural', but also other phenomena which, like sorcery, needed to be understood in some other way. It was a distinction that Ælfric clearly thought was shared among the members of his congregation as well – for if it were not, then it would hardly have helped him to explain the reasonableness of his views to them. Certainly in the surviving writings of other early medieval English men and women, we regularly find ideas about the world and its workings which are just as unfamiliar to us as Ælfric's. During this period, ecclesiastics could be found sharing

---

[1] Ælfric, *Catholic Homilies*, I.6 (ed. Clemoes, p. 230).
[2] Ælfric's immediate source was Bede, *De temporum ratione*, ch. 28 (ed. Jones, pp. 364–5), which was itself drawing upon Ambrose, *Exameron*, IV.7 (ed. Schenkl, pp. 134–5); Vegetius, *Epitoma rei militaris*, IV.35 (ed. Reeve, p. 148); and Eustathius's Latin translation of Basil of Caesarea's *Hexaemeron*, VI.10–11 (ed. de Mendieta and Rudberg, pp. 85–6). Ælfric returns to these ideas also in his *De temporibus anni* (ed. Blake, p. 90).
[3] Ælfric, *Catholic Homilies*, I.6 (ed. Clemoes, p. 230).

reports about people who had recently returned from the dead, filled with urgent news about the invisible activities of otherworldly beings more powerful than any creature which lived upon the earth.[4] Farmers whose fields had become unproductive could be shown how to undertake complex rituals to restore their land to fruitfulness, no matter what might previously have been done to it by harmful magic.[5] The users of medical remedy-books could learn that certain plants were especially useful against 'elf-sickness', but that one risked being disturbed by 'something terrifying' when one went to dig them out of the ground.[6]

It is easy enough to recognize from examples like these that early medieval English men and women understood their world very differently from the way that we understand ours. We face a more difficult challenge, however, when we attempt to convey and characterize those dissimilar views by means of the words and concepts that are available to us, but which may map imprecisely – if at all – onto those of the people whose ideas we are seeking to comprehend. Ought we conclude from ideas like the ones which I have just listed that 'the world of the early Middle Ages' was, as Caroline Walker Bynum suggests, one 'in which the supernatural may break into everyday life at any moment'?[7] Or might it in fact mean that early medieval men and women possessed, as Karen Louise Jolly has argued, a 'view of nature and knowledge that did not separate natural from supernatural' whatsoever, and therefore that 'the modern distinction between natural and supernatural did not exist at this time'?[8] And if that is so, then do we retain this terminology in our own studies only on the basis that it is 'sufficiently ensconced in the common cultural lexicon' of our own times, and can therefore be deployed even when we acknowledge it to be 'slightly anachronistic' to the period under investigation, as Stephen Gordon suggests?[9] Or if the people whose ideas we seek to understand could 'conceive of [no] entity defined by the exclusion of the supernatural', as Jennifer Neville has argued, then should we resist the temptation to bring 'convenient, anachronistic' categories into our analysis which might cloud the intended meaning of their words?[10]

In this Element, I want to examine the degree to which men and women in early medieval England did or did not conceive of a distinction between natural and supernatural. In their reflections about creatures and beings both common and uncommon (Section 1), in their understanding of innate properties and

---

[4] *Die Briefe*, X (ed. Tangl, pp. 8–15). [5] See Section 3.
[6] *Leechbook III*, ch. 62 (ed. Cockayne, vol. II, p. 346). [7] Bynum, *Jesus as Mother*, p. 12.
[8] Jolly, *Popular Religion*, p. 72; and Jolly, 'Anglo-Saxon charms', p. 281. See also Jolly, 'Father God'.
[9] Gordon, *Supernatural Encounters*, p. 12. [10] Neville, *Representations*, pp. 2–3.

behaviours (Section 2), and in their views about the different ways in which human beings could enact change through words, deeds, and actions (Section 3), we find indications of how early medieval English thinkers characterized and categorized the world around them. Their writings on these subjects not only offer us important insights into the intellectual and cultural conditions of their own society, but also hold implications for scholars of other places and periods as well, who have frequently sought to trace the history of our own concepts of 'the natural' and 'the supernatural', and to determine when and why those concepts may first have arisen. For some, like the French sociologist Émile Durkheim, they were inescapably modern and had been 'constructed little by little by the positive sciences' over the course of the nineteenth century.[11] We shall return to Durkheim's argument in support of this position in Section 2; but for now, we may note the existence, already in the Middle Ages, of the word *supernaturalis* ('supernatural') in a varied range of Latin texts dealing with theological matters. The development and spread of the term was mapped out almost a century ago by the Catholic theologian Henri de Lubac, who showed that it became common only from the thirteenth century onwards, in the hands of intellectuals who sought to distinguish certain types of events and phenomena from others which occurred *naturaliter* ('naturally').[12] One possible way of accounting for this new willingness of later medieval writers to talk in terms of the 'supernatural', in language that was not shared by their predecessors, would be to take it, as Alexander Murray has suggested, as an indication that they lived and worked in 'a new conceptual environment', adhering to patterns of thought that were not shared in earlier centuries.[13] It is however equally possible, as Robert Bartlett has observed, that the utility of the term for later medieval thinkers lay not so much in the fact that it allowed them 'to say something they could not say before', but simply that it allowed them to express much older and less innovative ideas 'more often and more conveniently'. Some explanation for their desire to do so might be sought, Bartlett suggests, in the contemporaneous development of newly formalized and bureaucratic processes for the canonization of saints, devised in order to assess the validity of claims about the purported sanctity of individuals whose deeds could be said to have operated 'above or contrary to nature', and which therefore supplied 'a new and very practical need that stimulated thinking about the distinction between the supernatural and the natural'.[14] Perhaps, therefore, the kinds of enquiries pursued by papal commissioners as part of the canonization process were merely more formal and precisely defined versions of much older

---

[11] Durkheim, trans. Swain, *Elementary Forms*, p. 28.   [12] De Lubac, *Surnaturel*, pp. 323–428.
[13] Murray, *Reason and Society*, p. 12.   [14] Bartlett, *The Natural and the Supernatural*, pp. 9–17.

ideas. Already in the schools of the twelfth century, the workings of the physical world were being distinguished from the direct operation of divine power, in what Marie-Dominique Chenu was content to characterize as a new and remarkable 'discovery of Nature'.[15] Yet Carl Watkins has subsequently shown that the schools were by no means a 'necessary precondition' for this way of thinking, and that 'rough-and-ready' distinctions between what was 'natural' and what was not were already being offered by writers unconnected to the schools and their new intellectual resources.[16] The pursuit after an originary moment for the concepts of 'natural' and 'supernatural' tends, in other words, to pull us backwards rather than forwards in time, as the intellectual developments of later centuries expand upon, rather than sharply break away from, ways of thinking that could indeed have been intelligible to the generations that preceded them.

My aim in this Element is to suggest that efforts to distinguish 'natural' from 'supernatural' phenomena were indeed undertaken in early medieval England, by men and women whose mode of expression necessarily differed from that of later centuries, but who deemed it possible nonetheless to differentiate between the 'natural' workings of their world and other forces which, they believed, might sometimes act upon it. As we shall see, our sources do not speak with a single voice on this issue and instead sometimes indicate that individuals could and did arrive at different conclusions about how to conceptualize the world in which they lived. Our goal cannot, therefore, be to pretend that we can (or should) simply draw up a list of what early medieval English men and women regarded as 'natural' and another of what they did not. My interest, instead, is to try to identify some of the contexts, needs, and situations which prompted contemporaries to pose questions about the categorization of phenomena, and to deem it useful or necessary to try to determine where the boundaries of the 'natural' ought to be drawn. It is by doing so, I would argue, that we can most clearly see their ideas as constituent parts of the social conditions in which they were generated, and by which they were sustained.

We are unavoidably better informed about some of these situations than others: the kinds of questions which mattered most to members of the institutional church are those which emerge most clearly in the surviving sources from the period. If equivalent conversations took place in the English kingdoms before their conversion to Christianity, we can often only guess; and even with the greater quantities of written texts produced during the centuries after conversion, the perspectives of lay Christians are typically less well-attested

---

[15] Chenu, *Nature, Man, and Society*, ed. and trans. Taylor and Little, pp. 4–18.
[16] Watkins, *History and the Supernatural*, pp. 18–20 and 33–5.

than those voiced by their ecclesiastical contemporaries. Nonetheless, precisely because ecclesiastics often sought to offer their opinions about these issues *to* the laity, commenting on aspects of their behaviour and anticipating the potential for disagreement or debate, we should resist the assumption that the things which were 'beyond nature' mattered only to the professional religious.[17] The case has been made on linguistic grounds that speakers of Old English were equipped with 'a substantial lexicon of the otherworldly', seen most especially in the range of compounds formed with the prefix *el-* ('foreign, strange; from elsewhere'), and ecclesiastical Latin was very much not, therefore, the only register in which the boundaries of 'nature' could be explored.[18] When Ælfric of Eynsham invited his late tenth-century congregation to reflect upon the 'natural things through Creation', and to set them against other kinds of practices and phenomena which seemed not to number among them, he assumed that he was speaking to people who were accustomed to seeing the difference. My aim in what follows is to sketch out some of the circumstances which were already prompting men and women in early medieval England to make equivalent distinctions of their own.

1 Creatures and Beings

Perhaps we should begin with a donkey. Early medieval readers of the Bible knew that there had once been an ancient diviner named Balaam, who was summoned by the king of Moab to curse the Israelites, but who became mysteriously unable to control the donkey on which he rode when he followed the Moabites back to their country (Figure 1). The animal had swerved off the road, then crushed its rider against a wall, and finally refused to move at all; and Balaam had beaten it angrily in his attempt to continue his journey. But God, in response, had 'opened the donkey's mouth' and enabled it to speak to Balaam, complaining about the cruelty and injustice of his treatment. The truth of the matter, as Balaam was soon shown, was not that the donkey had deliberately sought to ignore its master, but instead that it had been trying to keep him away from an angel which had been standing ahead, invisible to Balaam and armed with a sword to cut him down.[19]

Early in the eighth century, the Northumbrian monk Bede (d. 735) found himself summarizing this same story in one of his biblical commentaries. Its central message, Bede stated, was that error and foolishness might sometimes be revealed through the unlikeliest of channels. This, he observed, was a lesson that his fellow clerics would do well to remember, lest they presume that either

---

[17] In this connection, see also Foxhall Forbes, *Heaven and Earth*.
[18] Hall, *Elves*, pp. 11–12; Mearns, 'This, that and the other'. [19] Numbers 22.

Figure 1 Balaam and his donkey, in an unfinished illustration from the Old English Hexateuch (London, British Library, Cotton Claudius B.iv, fol. 126r). By permission of the British Library.

their profession or their learning made them immune from the criticism of humbler folk. Here was a story which showed that God might draw attention to human misdemeanours in any way he chose – even by making an example of a man by 'rebuking him by the words of a donkey that spoke, contrary to nature'.[20]

It is that last remark that we should stop to consider. Bede expressed no doubt that the animal really had spoken to Balaam, but its ability to do so had been *contra naturam* – contrary, that is, not only to the creature's own capacities but also to a fundamental distinction instituted at the Creation between humans and animals. Among all the living creatures which populated the terrestrial earth, Bede believed, only humans had been endowed by God with reason. This was for Bede, as for other Christian thinkers, such an absolute distinction between human and animal natures that he elsewhere emphasized that even the serpent in the Garden of Eden 'should not be thought to have had its mind changed [from an animal nature] to a rational nature', solely on the grounds that it was known once to have spoken to Eve before the Fall. More probably, Bede thought, it had been possessed by the Devil, and must itself have been 'unable to understood the sounds of the words which it made'.[21] Something altogether different had apparently happened to Balaam's donkey. The inherent natures of the creatures, forms, and substances which had been established by God in the unfolding of

---

[20] Bede, *In epistulas septem catholicas*, III.ii.15–16 (ed. Hurst, p. 274).
[21] Bede, *In Genesim*, I.iii.1 (ed. Jones, p. 60); quoting Augustine, *De Genesi ad litteram*, XI.28 (ed. Zycha, pp. 360–1).

his Creation were not regularly contravened; but they could nonetheless be changed, transformed, and made to behave differently, according to the will of God. Later in the same commentary, Bede observed that the things reported about Christ's body confirmed that it had possessed 'the true nature of flesh' in every regard, and yet simultaneously behaved in ways which acted 'contrary to the nature of bodies' (*contra naturam corporum*).[22] Biblical history demonstrated for Bede that the material realities of the created world could still be subject to startling interventions, wrought by the power which had first given them shape.

It was certainly possible in this period to find individuals willing to conceptualize the workings of God as being 'above nature' on the basis of precisely these sorts of biblical details. Contained within the acts of the Lateran synod of 649, for instance, were passing remarks about the way that the events of Christ's life – both the circumstances of his birth, and also the fact that 'unsteady water had supported the weight of his earthly and material feet without giving way' – showed the operation of 'a power above nature' (*supra naturam uirtus*, in the Latin text of the bilingual acts).[23] These statements were quoted from the writings of a man whom the compilers of the acts took to be Dionysius, first bishop of Athens, but who had in truth been a much more recent figure, working under that pseudonym around the start of the sixth century.[24] Pseudo-Dionysus was an author who was particularly given to philosophical statements that emphasized the paradoxical and the ineffable, and his writings were not yet widely available in the Latin West when they were put to use in the theological debates of the Lateran council; but readers who encountered them in the written acts of the council clearly found them consistent with their own views about the relationship between God and the material world. Bede in fact numbered among those readers and chose to quote from them himself in his own works, reaffirming with pseudo-Dionysius that the details of Christ's incarnation revealed the operation of something that was 'beyond the natural' (*praeter naturalem*).[25]

We should not take statements such as these to indicate that God was thought to work invariably or exclusively in ways that could be said to be 'above nature'. The regular operation of the world, with its familiar rhythms and everyday

---

[22] Bede, *In epistulas septem catholicas*, IV.v.7–8 (ed. Hurst, p. 321); and cf. also Bede, *Expositio actuum apostolorum*, II.19 (ed. Laistner, p. 19).
[23] *Concilium Lateranense* (649), III (ed. Riedinger, pp. 130–1). On the relationship of the Greek and Latin versions of the acts, and their debated relationship with the proceedings of the council itself, see Price, *Acts*, pp. 59–68.
[24] Pseudo-Dionysius, *Epistula* IV (ed. Heil and Ritter, pp. 160–1).
[25] Bede, *In Marci*, II.vi.50–51 (ed. Hurst, p. 518); quoting *Concilium Lateranense*, III (ed. Riedinger, p. 129), which itself quotes pseudo-Dionysius, *De diuinis nominibus*, 2.9 (ed. Suchla, p. 133).

occurrences, was no less a manifestation of divine will than any other act accomplished by the Creator. In his treatise *De natura rerum* ('On the Nature of Things'), Bede encouraged his readers to understand that 'the Father and the Son work right up to the present', and that they did so in everything that 'arises from the natural course of things'.[26] Drawing on ideas formulated by Augustine, bishop of Hippo (d. 430), Bede's treatise explained that the continuing operation of the divine will was to be found in the 'seeds and primordial causes' which God had implanted in his Creation at its beginning, and which had ever since unfolded in the manner which God had always intended, sustaining new life and underpinning its stable operation into the present.[27] One Old English poet was particularly struck by this way of thinking and sought to capture in verse the way that 'every day, through God's decree, the innate and life-animating powers bring many wonders to generations of men'.[28] His poem, which modern editors have entitled either *The Wonder of Creation* or *The Order of the World*, celebrated the immanence of God within the everyday phenomena of the material world. In it, the poet explained that everything in heaven and earth took place 'in just the way that the Steersman had commanded them'.[29] The result, for the poet, was that even something as apparently unremarkable as the rising and falling of the sun ought to be regarded as a source of great wonder, beyond the capacity of any person 'to investigate ... in their mind any further than the Lord has granted them to understand'.[30] Yet even here, in a poem which focused chiefly on the continual and ineffable presence of God in every part of his Creation, the poet was clear that divine agency in the material world was in no way limited to the mere unfolding of the primordial causes which God had instituted and left to unfold by themselves. Material phenomena might also, he said, have to be 'maintained by the necessary command of the holy Lord', who apparently continued therefore to act directly and regularly upon his Creation; and from the fact that 'these works do not weaken', the poet could conclude that 'he maintains [them] well' in the present day.[31] A conviction that the mundane realities of the visible world were wholly permeated by the mysterious power of the Creator who gave them shape was not, therefore, antithetical to a basic sense that God stood at the same time *beyond* his Creation in some way.

It may be true to say that late antique and early medieval writings about the relationship between God and his Creation were 'unconcerned with the

---

[26] Bede, *De natura rerum*, ch. 1 (ed. Jones, p. 192); cf. also *Homilia*, I.23 (ed. Hurst, p. 168). See further Wallis, '*Si naturam quæras*'.
[27] See Ahern, *Bede and the Cosmos*, pp. 56–61.
[28] *Wonder of Creation*, lines 5–7 (ed. Stanley, p. 479).
[29] *Wonder of Creation*, lines 45b–46 (ed. Stanley, p. 483).
[30] *Wonder of Creation*, lines 27–30 (ed. Stanley, p. 481).
[31] *Wonder of Creation*, lines 72–5 and 86–9 (ed. Stanley, pp. 484 and 493).

distinction between natural and supernatural' when they sought to argue, as Augustine and after him Bede did, that 'God works in the natural operation' of the world.[32] At the same time, however, they were careful not to suggest that the universe and its Creator were coterminous, and they affirmed that even if God did not necessarily act in ways that were 'contrary to nature' then nevertheless, as the fate of Balaam's donkey alone was sufficient to show, he also remained unconstrained by the ordinary rules of his Creation. We do not, I think, fundamentally distort these ideas if we express them in the language of 'natural' and 'supernatural', as long as we recognize when we do that early medieval men and women might find evidence of what pseudo-Dionysius had called 'the power above nature' even in places where we might not expect to see it.

These ideas not only informed the way in which early medieval Christians thought about their own religious traditions, but also how they responded to the beliefs of others. There were in this period a number of contexts in which Christians were in close contact with non-Christians, whose dissimilar views of the world and the beings which inhabited it could readily become the topic of debate. It was perhaps here that firm lines between 'natural' and 'supernatural' beings could most easily be drawn, in conversations which turned on the question of how to determine the validity of opposing belief-systems. One way in which such conversations might be conducted was sketched out for the English missionary Boniface (d. 754) by Daniel, bishop of Winchester (d. 745), in a letter which aimed to assist Boniface in converting 'the stony and barren hearts of the pagans' beyond the Rhine (Figure 2).[33] Although Boniface had already gained papal support for his missionary ambitions among these people, his efforts were still in their infancy when Daniel's letter arrived from England with ideas about how they might best be put into practice. Imagining himself in his countryman's position, Daniel advised Boniface to refrain at first from offering his own views to the pagans, and to ask them instead to offer him an account of their own gods. It was likely, Daniel suspected, that in that account the pagans would make genealogical comments about the interrelationship of their many gods, and to state 'that they had been begotten by others through the intercourse of male and female'. Daniel advised Boniface to seize upon such details, to put it to the pagans that their gods seemed to be possessed of no greater powers of creation than the humans who worshipped them, and thus to 'prove that gods and goddesses born in the manner of humans must indeed be humans, not gods'. Similar questions were to follow: if the gods' creative powers were so alike to the familiar processes of human procreation, then

---

[32] Ahern, 'Bede's miracles', p. 292. Augustine, *De ciuitate Dei*, XVI.26 (ed. Dombart and Kalb, vol. II, p. 530); Bede, *In Genesim*, IV.xvii.15–16 (ed. Jones, p. 207).

[33] *Die Briefe*, XXIII (ed. Tangl, pp. 38–41).

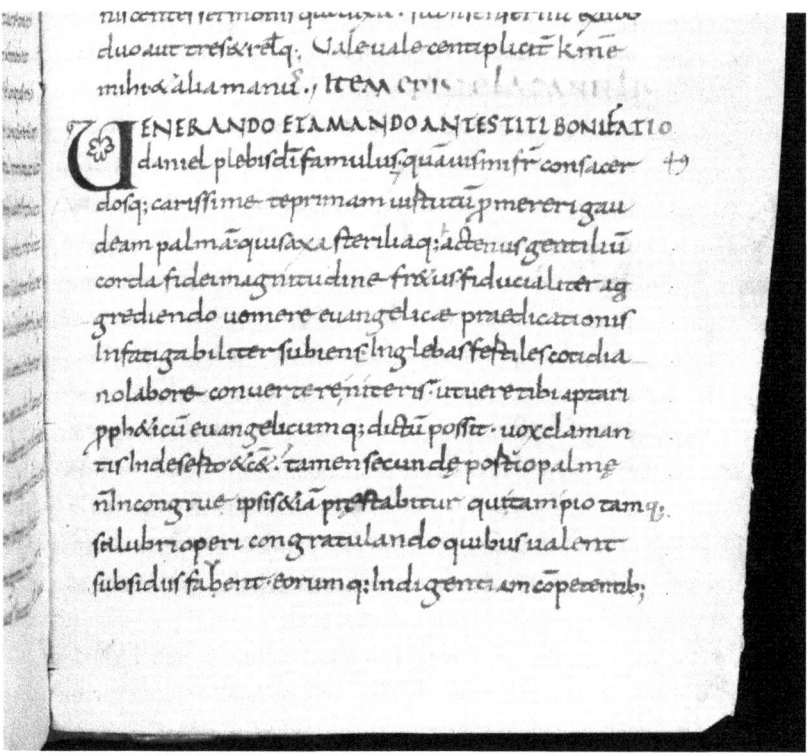

Figure 2 Daniel, bishop of Winchester, advises Boniface about methods of conversion (Karlsruhe, Badische Landesbibliothek, Cod. Rastatt 22, fol. 62r). By permission of the Badische Landesbibliothek.

surely that cast doubt on any possibility that they could have created the universe in which they lived – 'for without doubt', said Daniel, there was 'no place where gods engendered in this way could have supported themselves or resided *before* the creation of the universe'. What Daniel was outlining here was a line of questioning by which Boniface's pagans could be invited to consider the manner in which their gods interacted with the material facts of the world. His expectation was that Christians and non-Christians alike could find it meaningful to distinguish between those beings whose existence was dependent on a number of material preconditions – a line of ancestors, or a plane on which to dwell – and those which were instead believed to exist alongside, rather than within, the 'natural' rules of the universe. Boniface's task was to encourage the non-Christians with whom he spoke to conclude that the pagan gods were, in effect, insufficiently supernatural. Giving thought to the categorization of beings, in other words, struck Bishop Daniel as a fruitful method of engaging in debate with men and women who did not already share one's view of the world. He hoped that if Boniface was able to 'confuse rather than aggravate' his would-be converts in this way, by making them doubtful about certain aspects of their current beliefs, then this might open the way for Boniface to begin to instruct them in new doctrines derived from his own faith.

Bishop Daniel's letter offers only an imagined dialogue, and it may be that Boniface never in fact followed its script in his own conversations with non-Christians. If questions like Daniel's were indeed ever posed by Christian missionaries during the early Middle Ages, it may well be that the pagans with whom they spoke were better able to offer counter-arguments than Daniel assumed. The gods who were once worshipped in the English kingdoms before their own conversion to Christianity seem, for instance, to have been thought capable of affecting the behaviours and mental conditions of human beings. That much at least is suggested by the Old English word *gydig*, a term which survives now as Modern English 'giddy', but which originally denoted the state of being 'like one engaged with a god', and which continued to be used in both Old and Middle English to refer to individuals afflicted by madness, insanity, or other types of mental disturbances.[34] Here, one suspects, were ideas that could have been used to counter the proposition that non-Christian deities were just 'men and not gods', if that thought had ever been shared by the earlier missionaries who had contributed to the conversion of the English in the late sixth and seventh centuries.

It is significant, nonetheless, that Bishop Daniel should have begun his list of questions about the status of the pagan gods with matters of reproduction and generation. These were processes in which the whole of the physical world might be understood in some way to participate, and a number of early English writers saw them as central characteristics of the natural world in all its forms. It is to these themes, for instance, that Aldhelm, abbot of Malmesbury (d. 709), returned again and again in an extensive and influential collection of riddles, which number among his earliest surviving compositions. The one hundred individual riddles which make up his collection consider in turn an eclectic range of animals, plants, natural phenomena, and man-made objects. Although each of Aldhelm's riddles typically focuses upon a single creature or thing in isolation – a swallow, a cloud, a cask of wine, and so on – his collection as a whole presents the impression, as Michael Lapidge and James Rosier have emphasized, of a universe which 'is in a continual process of gestation, birth and growth'.[35] Readers of Aldhelm's riddles discover, for instance, that fires reminisce about their mothers and fathers, that minerals are created through the

---

[34] See Hall, *Elves*, p. 149 (with n. 102 for the proposed definition).
[35] Lapidge and Rosier, *Aldhelm*, pp. 63–6.

transformation of other elements, and that carved spindles might still recall the green forests in which their material substance was first born:

> 'A father and a mother produced me from icy numbness, and my beginnings were vigorous then, while the kindling was dry ...'[36]
>
> 'Once I was water, overflowing with scaly fish, but that nature yielded to a new decision of fate ...'[37]
>
> 'I was born in a forest glade, growing green on a forking bough, but in due course, fortune changed my fate, so that now I carry a rounded stone which whirls about my neck ...'[38]

As the examples multiplied, they brought out ever more strongly how each of the constituent parts of the material world was connected with others. Aldhelm's riddles ask their readers to consider the complex ecological or artisanal interrelationships that bind together even the most unlikely of things – how the poisonous flesh of serpents nourishes the fragile bodies of young birds; how the tiniest insects prey upon the largest and most aggressive creatures when they draw blood from their powerful muscles; or how a dagger, if endowed with thought, might acknowledge the many different species of animals which had died to provide the leather in which it was now enclosed.[39] Although Aldhelm could rightly say that his riddles drew attention to 'the varied qualities of things', his collection nonetheless indicated the degree to which every aspect of the material world seemed to be bound up in the *same* shared processes of birth, death, consumption, and generation.[40] These were images which resonated with other early English writers too. Towards the end of the eighth century, the Northumbrian deacon Alcuin (d. 804) could be found giving much the same sense of the things that characterized material existence in an educational *Disputatio* addressed to a young Frankish prince named Pippin (d. 810). There, in answer to the question 'What is the earth?' (*Quid est terra?*), Alcuin brought out the same fundamental connections between the processes of birth, destruction, and consumption as Aldhelm had done a century earlier. The earth, he said, could be understood as 'the mother of the growing, the nurse of the living, the storeroom of life, and the devourer of all things'.[41]

Despite Alcuin's remark that 'all things' could be understood according to their relationship with these generative processes, he and his contemporaries nevertheless often found themselves speculating about forms of life which were

---

[36] Aldhelm, *Enigmata*, XLIV (ed. Ehwald, p. 116).
[37] Aldhelm, *Enigmata*, XIX (ed. Ehwald, p. 105).
[38] Aldhelm, *Enigmata,* XLV (ed. Ehwald, p. 117).
[39] Aldhelm, *Enigmata*, XXXI, XXXVI, and LXI (ed. Ehwald, pp. 110–11, 113, and 125).
[40] Aldhelm, *Epistola ad Acircium*, ch. 5 (ed. Ehwald, p. 75).
[41] Alcuin, *Disputatio Pippini*, 56 (ed. Suchier, p. 140).

neither nursed upon the earth nor destined to be swallowed up by it. An 'invisible and spiritual creation' stretched out beyond the 'corporeal, visible, and corruptible creation' in which humankind dwelt. That was the way that Bede distinguished between the different parts of the universe, and he intended his words to convey the degree to which that 'invisible and spiritual creation' had been 'kept apart from every condition of this inconstant world' (Figure 3).[42] Those familiar facts of birth, death, reproduction, and material sustenance which Aldhelm and Alcuin had emphasized in their treatment of earthly life pertained not at all to the sorts of beings which inhabited the spiritual creation. When early medieval homilists sought, for instance, to instruct their congregations about angels – immaterial beings thought to dwell in their multitudes in the heavens – they remarked upon the mysterious way in which these incorporeal beings experienced 'neither corruption nor diminution' in their deathless existence.[43] Ecclesiastical writers frequently took the opportunity to hypothesize about the various ways in which creatures of these kinds differed from those which inhabited the earth. They speculated, for instance, about whether spiritual beings possessed different powers of perception to those of humans or animals, unmediated as they were by the material organs of the body.[44] They examined

Figure 3 The visible and invisible creations, in the illustration to Psalm 8 from the Harley Psalter (London, British Library, Harley 603, fol. 4v). By permission of the British Library.

---

[42] Bede, *In Genesim*, I.i.2 (ed. Jones, pp. 4 and 7).

[43] Helisachar of Trier, *Legimus in ecclesiasticis historiis* (ed. Cross, pp. 107–8); and later Ælfric, *Catholic Homilies*, I.36 (ed. Clemoes, p. 486). On the attribution of the Latin sermon to Helisachar, see Rauer, 'Female hagiography', pp. 24–5.

[44] E.g. *Die Briefe*, X (ed. Tangl, p. 8).

biblical stories about incorporeal angels and demons manifesting themselves upon the earth, and they theorized about how and why they could possess physical bodies in order to do so, and what might happen if they consumed material food while clothed in that form.[45] They wondered too if the spiritual creation might be home not only to angels and demons but also to more ambiguous creatures which resembled them in their deathless eternity, like the strange worm-like beings said by some to dwell 'undyingly' in the pits of hell.[46]

Early medieval Christians were firm in their conviction that there existed beyond the material world a whole host of beings which differed markedly from those which populated the earth. Yet spiritual creatures remained creatures nonetheless, as preachers were quick to remind their congregations, and in that sense they were just as 'natural' as anything which one might encounter in the physical world. They numbered among the works of God, and it was from him that they had been endowed with 'natures' of their own, even if it remained 'for God alone to know how their invisible nature [*ungesewenlice gecynd*] is sustained', as one of Ælfric of Eynsham's sermons put it.[47] To consider them in terms of their essential creatureliness was an important way of rendering them comprehensible, through analogy and comparison with the familiar creatures of the material world. When Ælfric informed his congregation that 'no creature is capable of fully contemplating or perceiving God', for instance, he emphasized that this was true not only of earthly creatures, but also of the angels, which were 'closer to God than humans are, and yet nevertheless are not able to perceive God completely'.[48]

One reason that Ælfric thought it necessary to insist upon the creatureliness of spiritual beings was that he suspected that some among his listeners might be in danger of overlooking it. There were, he said, people who were willing to entertain the possibility that God was not the sole creator of the material world, and that some parts of it had been fashioned instead by the Devil.[49] Ælfric was unspecific about who precisely may have held this opinion ('foolish men' he said in one place; 'heretics' in another), but he understood this to be how some people explained why many dangerous species of wild animals exhibited such ferocity towards human beings. Ælfric was unsurprisingly scornful of the idea and informed his congregation that the Devil 'can create no creatures, for he is not a creator'. It was accepted in his day that even if

---

[45] See Ahern, *Bede and the Cosmos*, pp. 126–50.
[46] See Millard, 'Significance of the *wyrm*', pp. 190–210.
[47] Ælfric, *Catholic Homilies*, I.36 (ed. Clemoes, p. 486), drawing closely upon Helisacher, *Legimus in ecclesiasticis historiis* (ed. Cross, pp. 107–8).
[48] Ælfric, *Catholic Homilies*, I.1 (ed. Clemoes, pp. 178–9); cf. also *Catholic Homilies*, I.20 (p. 336).
[49] Ælfric, *Catholic Homilies*, I.1 and I.6 (ed. Clemoes, pp. 182–3 and 230).

spiritual beings possessed no creative powers of their own, then nevertheless they might be capable of *affecting* the material things of the visible world, and perhaps did so routinely at the behest of the Creator. According to one set of blessings copied into a Northumbrian servicebook during the tenth century, for instance, there were 'forty-four thousand angels set over all the fruits of the earth and over seeds'; and readers of patristic theology could find similarly enthusiastic declarations there about the way that 'every visible thing in the world is placed under angelic power'.[50] As to what this power accomplished, and how it was exercised, some writers in this period seem to have thought that it was capable of altering the propensities or dispositions of other beings. In the Old English poem known as *Guthlac A*, for instance, particular attention is given to the relationship between its hero, the Mercian hermit St Guthlac (d. 714), and the guardian angel who came eventually to watch over him. Guthlac was one of those holy souls who had abandoned a life of worldly glory and instead chosen to 'dwell in desolate places' far from the company of human beings, but supported instead by angels who 'stand before them ready with the weapons of spirits and mindful of their safety; they preserve the life of holy people'.[51] Their support had been granted to Guthlac too – but only *after* he had turned his back on the world, insisted the Old English poet telling Guthlac's tale. A time had been appointed 'when God, in his wisdom, would give an angel to Guthlac so that his lust for sin would subside in him'; and the result, said the poet, was that this man who had once 'loved many perilous things' during his secular youth came to experience the world in new ways. He imagined the saint's mental and physical responses being fundamentally altered by the angel's arrival, and described his hermit-saint marvelling about the way that 'cravings come upon me only a little, and anxieties hardly at all, now that a spiritual shepherd watches over me'.[52] Remarks such as these bring us closer to a view of spiritual beings that we could justifiably call 'supernatural', in their willingness to suggest that certain kinds of creatures had the power to effect change upon the bodies and behaviours of others.

Early medieval writings about God's spiritual creations pull, therefore, in two different directions at once, sometimes giving particular attention to the 'naturalness' of invisible beings by appealing to their essential creatureliness, while at other times attributing to them the sort of power over the natures of other things which more closely resembled that of their Creator. We should not, I think, feel

---

[50] *Rituale ecclesiae Dunelmensis*, ed. Lindelöf, p. 146; on which see Sowerby, *Angels*, pp. 207–11. Augustine, *De diuersis quaestionibus*, ch. 79 (ed. Mutzenbecher, p. 225).
[51] *Guthlac A*, lines 81–92, ed. Roberts, *Guthlac Poems*, p. 85.
[52] *Guthlac A*, lines 108–13 and 316–18a, ed. Roberts, *Guthlac Poems*, pp. 86 and 92; see also Sowerby, *Angels*, pp. 85–7.

that we have to determine which of these tendencies deserves our greater emphasis, but instead simply recognize that early medieval Christians were here confronting a spectrum of opinion, from which different individuals must have drawn different conclusions about how best to think about the invisible beings with which they shared their world. Although contemporaries did not express this as a choice between a 'natural' and a 'supernatural' view of spiritual beings, that was in effect the matter at hand; and as Ælfric of Eynsham indicated, in his comments about the views which he thought some people held about the Devil, it was possible to arrive at opinions which brought one into conflict with others who saw the same matter differently.

That must have been especially true when individuals gave thought to the existence of creatures which could be found nowhere in the Bible, but which belonged instead to the spoken traditions of early medieval England. Those traditions become visible to us only in part, when they intersect with text; and often those textual traces are brief and highly allusive. A runic inscription scratched onto a small sheet of lead, recently discovered in Norfolk, declares that 'the dwarf is dead' but says nothing more about the circumstances which had necessitated the recording of that fact (Figure 4).[53] A book of medical remedies offers instructions about what to do 'if a *mære* should ride a person', identifying ingredients which might prove efficacious against this particular creature's attacks but saying nothing more about what exactly it might be.[54] Old English poets occasionally said that certain people were 'as beautiful as an elf' (*ælfscyne*), and thought that their audiences would know which qualities were exemplified by such a creature without further explication.[55] Ideas about these sorts of non-human beings had their origins in ideas which were already old by the time that they entered our sources, and which were also shared to some degree by speakers of other Germanic languages across north-western Europe, who possessed cognate words in their own languages for many of these same creatures (so for Old English *dweorg* 'dwarf', for instance, compare Old Norse *dvergr*, Old Frisian *dwerch*, Old High German *twerg*, and so on). They have always been valued by historians for the insights they might therefore provide about the beliefs which were current in the English-speaking kingdoms (and elsewhere) before the spread of Christianity in the sixth and seventh centuries. Their appearance in a wide variety of texts produced long after the conversion period nonetheless indicates the degree to which they could remain meaningful to English men and women in those later Christian centuries too. The person

---

[53] See Hines, 'Practical runic literacy', pp. 36–40.
[54] *Bald's Leechbook*, I.64 (ed. Cockayne, vol. II, p. 140). For other attestations, see Hall, 'Evidence'.
[55] See Hall, *Elves*, pp. 88–95.

Figure 4 Lead plaque found near Fakenham (Norfolk), bearing the inscription 'The dwarf is dead'. Adapted from images © Norfolk County Council, licensed under CC BY-SA 4.0.

who thought it necessary to record – or to hope – that 'the dwarf is dead' by inscribing it into a piece of lead clearly did not regard the existence of such beings as a matter of merely antiquarian interest; and this person seems, on the basis of their script, to have undertaken their task no earlier (and perhaps even a good deal later) than the middle of the eighth century.[56] To credit the existence of creatures of this sort need not have signified anything at all about an individual's wider religious beliefs, and it is in texts produced in the Christian kingdoms of early medieval England that we now encounter these inherited but still dynamic ideas about the wide variety of beings with which men and women thought they shared their world.

It is nevertheless clear that early medieval Christians could and did arrive at different conclusions about how best to make sense of these old ideas in light of the established teachings of the new faith. Some took the view that it must have been easy for earlier generations to fall victim to the deception of demons, when they lacked the resources of scripture and doctrine to guide their judgements about the world and its workings; and perhaps that meant that many of the

---

[56] Hines, 'Practical runic literacy', p. 40.

beings in which pre-Christian peoples had been willing to believe were really just demons, given different names by men and women who had been unable to recognize their true nature. This was an argument which was most readily deployed in connection with pagan gods, and English missionaries were among those who propagated it during this period. It appears, for instance, in the surviving text of a short baptismal vow which shows signs of English influence but which was evidently intended in its present form for use in a missionary context on the Continent, and which asked candidates to affirm that they had 'forsaken all the Devil's works and words', including the gods 'Thunar and Woden and Saxnot, and all those evil beings which are their associates'.[57] Formulations of this kind were unspecific about how wide the circle of 'evil beings' ought to be drawn, but some early medieval Christians clearly thought that it extended beyond gods and applied equally to the lesser creatures of vernacular myth. This must have been the view of the person who thought it prudent, in the middle of a protective prayer which survives now in an English prayerbook from around the year 800, to offer an adjuration against 'satanae diabulus aelfae' – a rather enigmatic statement which would seem to refer to the depredations of 'a devil of the elf Satan', in an unusual but nonetheless emphatic expression of equivalence between elves and demons.[58] A persistent strand of ecclesiastical opinion could be found making the same connection right through the Middle Ages, and indeed beyond.[59]

Although the demonological argument was to prove tenacious, it was not the only way in which traditional ideas about the existence of creatures such as elves or dwarves might be re-evaluated in light of Christian categories and cosmologies. One alternative was to look to biblical accounts of human history, and so to posit connections with other kinds of *physical* beings instead. That was the view expressed in the Old English poem *Beowulf*, as it peered into the moors and fens, asking its audience to imagine them populated by a multitude of 'misbegotten things', some encountered in terrifying detail in the poem, and others barely glimpsed around its edges. All of them owed their existence to the same ancient crime. The poet recalled for his audience the biblical account of the death of Adam and Eve's son Abel at the hands of his brother, whom God had then swiftly punished. Abel's brother, said the poet, 'was exiled for that crime, far from mankind; and thence sprang forth all misbegotten things: ogres and elves and dread creatures, as well as the giants which contended against

---

[57] Gysseling (ed.), *Corpus van Middelnederlandse teksten: Fragmenten*, p. 26. The text poses a number of interpretative challenges, for which see Mostert, 'Communicating the faith'.

[58] *Prayer Book*, ed. Kuypers, p. 221. For discussion, see Hall, *Elves*, pp. 71–2.

[59] See Green, *Elf Queens*, pp. 14–28.

God for a long while'.[60] Strands of exegetical interpretation about the existence and origins of monstrous creatures lie behind the poet's statement here, as a number of studies have indicated, and scholars as well as poets could be found expressing equivalent views in this period.[61] They sometimes grappled openly with the theological conundrums posed by such an opinion, as the author of a Middle Irish historical text known as the *Sex aetates mundi* ('The Six Ages of the World') did when he asked whether the things 'that the Irish say' about the monstrous progeny of Abel's brother, Cain, were compatible with the knowledge that there still were still believed to exist 'misshapen creatures' even after the biblical Flood in the days of Noah, which had surely succeeded in ensuring that 'none of his progeny survived the deluge'.[62] The connection between strange creatures and Cain's murder of Abel was nonetheless sufficiently well known that St Guthlac's hagiographer, Felix, could gesture towards it with only a passing allusion, when he said that the saint had once been tormented in the English marshes during the eighth century by a collection of evil creatures which he saw fit to refer to as 'the seed of Cain'.[63] The *Beowulf*-poet's account of the origin of 'misbegotten things' takes us not, therefore, into a world of purely literary imagination, but into a reasonably well-established area of contemporary thought which took seriously the existence – not only long ago, but also here and now – of a whole host of unusual beings at the edges of human society. Precisely what resemblance 'ogres and elves and dread creatures' bore to regular human forms as a result of their ancestral connection was ambiguous, even when they erupted startlingly out of the wild places and into the sight of others. The complicated picture which *Beowulf* presents of Grendel and his mother, whose attacks upon the royal hall of Heorot propel much of the action in the first part of the poem, derives much of its enigmatic power from the way that it positions them at one moment 'far from humankind', as 'alien spirits' (*ellorgæstas*) from 'the domain of the monster-race' (*fīfelcynnes eard*), while at the next allowing us to glimpse them 'in the likeness of a woman [and] the form of a man', animated by motivations that remain recognizably human.[64] The 'intentional, unresolvable' ambiguity of their depiction in *Beowulf* offered one poetic response to questions about the categorization and classification of

---

[60] *Beowulf*, lines 99–114 (ed. Klaeber, p. 5); and cf. also lines 1258b–67a (p. 48). Although both passages refer to the killing of Abel, there is some question as to whether the poet named the creatures' progenitor as Cain or as Cham: see Orchard, *Pride and Prodigies*, pp. 69–79; Neidorf, 'Cain', pp. 601–15.

[61] Carney, *Studies*, pp. 102–14; Peltola, 'Grendel's descent from Cain'; Mellinkoff, 'Cain's monstrous progeny' (Parts I and II); Orchard, *Pride and Prodigies*, pp. 58–85; Neidorf, 'Cain', pp. 608–15.

[62] *Sex aetates mundi*, chs. 17 and 34 (ed. Ó Cróinín, pp. 71 and 79); on which, see Clarke, 'Lore'.

[63] Felix, *Vita Guthlaci*, ch. 31 (ed. Colgrave, p. 106).

[64] *Beowulf*, lines 99–114 and 1345–61a (ed. Klaeber, pp. 5 and 51).

beings that were clearly of substantial interest to a wide variety of others in this period.[65]

A densely populated universe thus becomes visible to us in the written remains of early medieval England, filled with a greater diversity of beings and creatures than we ourselves typically imagine. We have sometimes taken that diversity as an indication that men and women in early medieval England would have deemed it 'impossible to distinguish between "natural" and "supernatural" phenomena' if, as Jennifer Neville has argued, we find in their writings that 'devilish sea-monsters (*niceras*), whales, wolves, demons (*þyrsas*), deer, blood-thirsty, man-shaped creatures (the Grendelkin), birds' all nevertheless 'inhabit the same landscapes and interact with human beings in parallel ways'.[66] Certainly, they found nothing unlikely in the idea that demons might sometimes be found in the same fields in which farmers grazed their cattle, or that the sounds heard on a hilltop monastery at night might turn out on one evening to be the calling of a cockerel, and on another to be the unearthly music of spirits travelling down from the stars.[67]

But although people might encounter them in the same places, the *manner* in which different sorts of creatures interacted with the world around them was not necessarily identical in every instance. We are meant, I think, to see something abnormal in Grendel's reported capacity not only to hide away in darkness, but also to manipulate his surroundings in order to do so: when 'he lurked and plotted', the *Beowulf*-poet said, he did so while 'holding the misty moors in unending night'.[68] Some indication that the poet meant that quite literally comes from the fact that he followed that statement immediately with the observation that 'men do not know where witches wend their way', deploying what Leonard Neidorf and Kexin Zhang have persuasively argued is 'a traditional gnomic statement on the inscrutability of beings that disregard human norms'.[69] Grendel, in other words, had passed not only beyond human sight as he slunk away, but also wholly beyond human understanding in the midst of that 'unending night' which he held upon his lair.

Other strange creatures described by writers in early medieval England appear equally unconstrained by the usual behaviour of their physical surroundings, according to reports which located them not in the distant lands of a poetic past as *Beowulf* does, but also in the living memory of well-informed English

---

[65] O'Brien O'Keeffe, '*Beowulf*, lines 702b–836', p. 489.
[66] Neville, *Representations*, pp. 2 and 118, n. 128.
[67] Demons and cattle: *Old English Dialogues*, ed. Anlezark, p. 74. Birds and spiritual choirs: Æthelwulf, *De abbatibus*, lines 659–94 (ed. Campbell, pp. 53–5).
[68] *Beowulf*, lines 161b–162a (ed. Klaeber, p. 7).
[69] Neidorf and Zhang, 'Grendel and the witches'.

witnesses. In the summer of 971, a man from Winchester encountered three terrifying creatures on the banks of the river Itchen. His story was recorded within a few years at most of the purported events by a Frankish monk named Lantfred (fl. 974–84), who said that the creatures had appeared in the shape of 'two raven-like women, no larger than the height of a human being' and 'a third one, amazingly tall, who stood like a tower over the others'.[70] Lantfred's report left open the question of exactly *what* these creatures might have been and chose instead, as Christopher Jones has shown, to make 'learned but finally non-committal reference' to a range of analogies drawn from classical myth and hagiographical legend, without ever fully settling upon any single way of interpreting what it was that the man from Winchester had seen.[71] Whatever they were, their surroundings could hardly have been more ordinary, with familiar pastureland in one direction and the city walls in the other, along a route which the man had often walked to inspect his livestock. But in amongst these familiar surroundings, Lantfred's three creatures come and go by strange and unusual means. They eventually disappear by 'casting themselves headlong into the stream of the river with a mighty leap', impeded in no way by the enormous size of their leader, so large that she had previously found it necessary to hide behind a hill in order to shield herself from view.[72]

In Lantfred's report, as in *Beowulf*, we are encouraged to imagine 'the inscrutability of beings that disregard human norms', and which interacted with their physical surroundings in ways that were beyond the capability of more familiar creatures. Early medieval men and women knew that birds in a storm, for instance, could choose only between flying 'up over the clouds in stormy weather, so that the storms cannot harm them', or otherwise simply sitting through it until the weather broke, 'calling out with rain-soaked feathers' from their perches.[73] They knew that a mighty whale that swam like a 'king of terror' in the open waters of the ocean was nevertheless powerless if it were to be washed ashore; and after they had made a box from its bones, they inscribed upon it their recognition that the mighty creature had ended its life only in grief, 'becoming sad where it swam on the sand'.[74] They spoke with precision about

---

[70] Lantfred, *Translatio*, ch. 3 (ed. Lapidge, pp. 274–6). [71] See Jones, 'Furies'.

[72] Lantfred, *Translatio*, ch. 3 (ed. Lapidge, p. 276). Some of Lantfred's wording resembles Virgil's description of Turnus's escape from a Trojan raid (see Jones, 'Furies', pp. 418–19), but if this offered Lantfred a partial model, then nonetheless he stops short of indicating that the departure of his creatures precisely matched that of Virgil's human fugitive: where Virgil follows Turnus as he is carried along by the current, Lantfred offers only the abrupt disappearance of a creature whose immense dimensions he had previously taken care to describe in some detail (see Jones, 'Furies', p. 426).

[73] *Old English Boethius* (B-text), ch. 7 (ed. Godden and Irvine, vol. I, p. 254). *Seafarer*, lines 23–5a, ed. Muir, *Exeter Anthology*, vol. I, p. 230.

[74] See Cavell, 'Community of exiles', pp. 100–103.

the habitats in which creatures could and could not dwell, regarding them as constrained by whatever 'nature allows' for them (*natura sinit*).[75] When early medieval writers then also told detailed and captivating stories about creatures which seemed to be unconstrained by any such considerations, either in their imaginative literature or in their accounts of reportedly real-life experiences, their words drew attention precisely to the aspects of their stories which were hardest to accommodate within their understanding of the 'normal' operation of the world. We have sometimes been told that a 'medieval discovery of Nature' lay still some way ahead in this period, and indeed that 'Nature's main lesson' for attentive men and women during those later centuries was that it was possible for them to 'see ... the difference between naturalistic and supernatural events', in a way that would have been incomprehensible for earlier generations.[76] On the basis of the kinds of stories which were already being told in early medieval England, though, we are permitted to wonder whether some of their early medieval predecessors had not already learned that lesson for themselves.

2 Properties and Processes

We saw in the Introduction that one of the arguments which has been made against the premodern applicability of 'the idea of the supernatural' is that we should properly understand it as a by-product of the development of the sciences. 'In order to say that certain things are supernatural', Émile Durkheim argued in the early part of the twentieth century, 'it is necessary to have the sentiment that a *natural order of things* exists, that is to say, that the phenomena of the universe are bound together by necessary relations, called laws'. In Durkheim's view, this way of understanding the operation of the universe had arisen only in modernity. It was, he argued, 'a conquest of the positive sciences' as they had developed during the nineteenth century and was therefore 'of recent origin; even the greatest thinkers of classical antiquity never succeeded in becoming fully conscious of it'. To expect premodern societies to have conceived of the world in terms of 'natural' and 'supernatural' phenomena was, for Durkheim, to expect them to have conformed to ways of thinking that simply 'could not have existed' long before his own day.[77]

The English cleric who composed a Life of St Dunstan towards the end of the tenth century was certainly no scientist. He is known to us now only as 'B.', the letter by which he referred to himself in the opening dedication of the Life, and

---

[75] Aldhelm, *Enigmata*, XXXVIII (ed. Ehwald, p. 114). See Sorrell, 'Like a duck to water'.
[76] Epstein, *Medieval Discovery of Nature*, p. 184.
[77] Durkheim, trans. Swain, *Elementary Forms*, pp. 26–8.

he had obtained his early education at the monastery of Glastonbury during the period in which Dunstan (d. 988) had served as its abbot. He was nonetheless comfortable with the idea that there were some things in this world which exhibited fundamental regularities. He was even content to characterize those regularities as 'laws'. It was through his consideration of human death that B. expressed that view. An eternal reward had surely been set aside for Dunstan in the heavens, said B., and the saint had gone to claim it when his bodily existence came to an end, in accordance with 'the age-old laws of death' (*leges auitae mortis*).[78]

The sentiment may not have been particularly deeply considered. It seems to have been B's habit to avoid 'say[ing] humdrum things in an obvious way', and whenever his narrative required him to note that a certain person had predeceased Dunstan, he regularly did so in language that was deliberately ornate or evocative.[79] But perhaps that only makes it more telling that the language of laws should have suggested itself to B. as he was casting around for an appropriate way of expressing what happened at the end of a person's life. His choice of words mirrors to some degree the impression given by contemporary sermons, which were often full of assurances about the experiences which awaited human souls as they passed from the body and entered into a new mode of existence. The precise nature of those assurances frequently varied from one sermon-writer to the next, in ways which have always made it easy for modern scholars to draw attention to the 'inconsistency' of theological opinion which they represent.[80] But those inconsistencies become most readily apparent when we collect a number of different sermons together and examine their handling of common themes. The men and women who heard any one of them being delivered were not necessarily in a position to engage in a similar act of comparison, and must often have been struck instead by the tone of emphatic certainty with which individual sermons typically delivered their messages. To hear it said that 'whether a person is truthful or untruthful, rich or poor, two angels will come for his soul', or to be given concrete details about the shape, colour, and appearance of the 'various forms' through which the bodies and souls of the dead would one day pass, was to be presented with a confident sense that the process of death conformed to regular, known patterns.[81] Many of the men and women who sat in a church and listened to sermons of this kind must

---

[78] B., *Vita Dunstani*, ch. 38 (ed. Winterbottom and Lapidge, pp. 107–9).
[79] Winterbottom and Lapidge, *Early Lives of St Dunstan*, pp. cxviii–cxix.
[80] See, for example, Gatch, 'Eschatology'.
[81] Angels: Bazire and Cross (eds.), *Rogationtide Homilies*, p. 121 [homily IX]; and see Sowerby, *Angels*, pp. 134–44. Posthumous transformations: *Vercelli Homilies*, ed. Scragg, pp. 96–7 and 101–2 [homily IV]; and see Hall, 'Psychedelic transmogrification'.

have been inclined to agree with St Dunstan's hagiographer, B., that there did indeed seem to be 'age-old laws of death', the operation of which was evidently well known to the preachers who were so eager to share what they knew with others.

Regularities and inevitabilities frequently drew comment from early English writers, for whom they were both utterly commonplace and profoundly significant. They were to be found everywhere, from the tiny transformation of fallen leaves mouldering into dust upon the ground, to the vast motions of celestial bodies wheeling across the night sky. A deep familiarity with their rhythms and recurrences could be depended upon by poets and moralists, who often used them to anchor more abstracted lessons about human life – like the reminders offered in an Old English poem known as *Solomon and Saturn II* about the transience of wealth and the inevitable doom of those who 'persist for a long time' in accumulating it, which the poet sought to express by ruminating upon the inexorable fate of decaying autumn leaves.[82] In the unchanging regularity of observable phenomena, the faithful hoped, some glimpse could be caught of the divine will that had first given them shape and set them in motion. Recurring and cyclical behaviours could be followed back through time, as they continued to obey in the present exactly the same 'rule[s] of association that [they] had previously received' from God, as Bede expressed it in the course of his own investigation into the conjoined movements of the moon and the tide.[83] And if this was so, then resemblances *between* the regular behaviours of different phenomena might prove to be highly significant, indicating something about the larger design of the universe as God had conceived it. Religious scholars eagerly mapped out the extent of these resemblances by superimposing them, one upon another, to make visible their interconnections and commonalities. The energy with which such efforts were made is particularly clear in the *Enchiridion* ('Handbook') produced by the studious Ramsey monk Byrhtferth (d. c. 1020) early in the eleventh century. Alongside his written exposition, Byrhtferth offered his readers a series of diagrams, which gave visible shape to the structures and rhythms at work within Creation (Figure 5). The lines of Byrhtferth's diagrams took in human bodies, their stages of life, the elements, the months and seasons, establishing points of connection between microcosm and macrocosm. Byrhtferth characterized the intended result of his labours as analogous to 'touching with our oars the waves of the deep water', and

---

[82] *Solomon and Saturn II*, lines 136–44, ed. Anlezark, *Old English Dialogues*, pp. 84–6; see also Hill, 'Falling leaf'.

[83] Bede, *De temporum ratione*, ch. 29 (ed. Jones, p. 371); and see Wallis, '*Si naturam quæras*', pp. 82–90.

expressed his conviction that through investigation and contemplation, the mind could begin to discern the true shape of the world which had been 'arranged, like holy scripture says, "in measure, and number, and weight"'.[84]

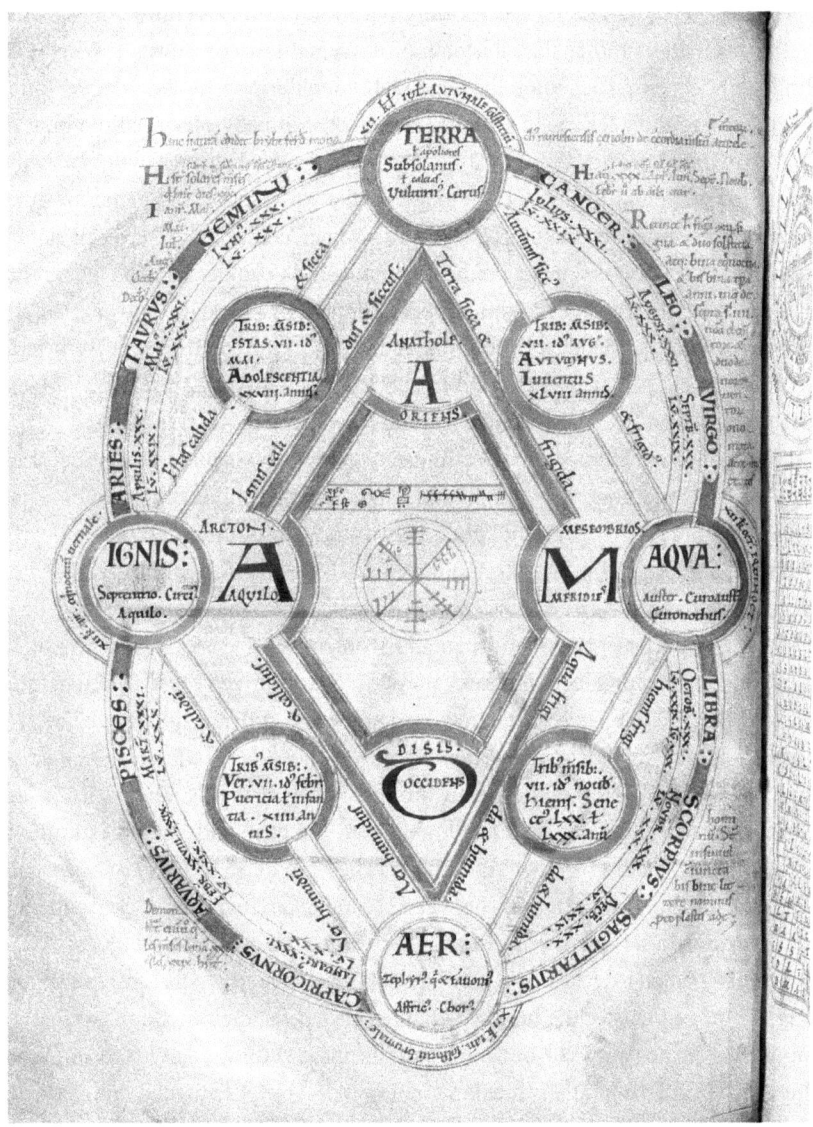

Figure 5 Connections between the microcosm and the macrocosm, mapped out by Byrhtferth of Ramsey (Oxford, St John's College, MS 17, fol. 7v). By permission of the President and Fellows of St John's College, Oxford.

---

[84] Byrhtferth, *Enchiridion*, I.1 (ed. Baker and Lapidge, pp. 6 and 16); and in reference to Wisdom 11:21.

These are not quite the 'necessary relations' between observable phenomena to which Durkheim had attached such importance, even if early writers showed themselves just as willing as he to describe them occasionally as 'laws'. Premodern expressions of the orderliness of the universe often rooted themselves, as Lorraine Daston has recently put it, in the consideration of 'specific and local natures rather than systems of universal laws or rules'.[85] When Old English poets remarked upon the dependably regular way in which many kinds of trees shed their leaves in autumn, as we have already observed the poet of *Solomon and Saturn II* doing, they did so on the basis that it was in the specific nature of particular kinds of trees to act in this way (and in the nature of other kinds of trees not to do so). The pursuit in later centuries of 'laws of nature [which] were universal in scope', and which could be understood as 'general in the sense of uniformity, holding everywhere and always' in any part of the universe, should indeed be differentiated from the kind of effort that Byrhtferth of Ramsey exerted in search of correspondences between the microcosm and the macrocosm.[86]

We should nonetheless be careful not to carry too far this contrast between modern and premodern ways of understanding the universe. Durkheim had suggested not only that premodern views of the world differed to some degree from modern ones, but more importantly that this therefore indicated that 'the sentiment that a *natural order of things* exists' must also necessarily have been absent. Yet even if premodern men and women saw the world in terms of an array of 'specific and local natures', they still characterized those varied natures in terms that emphasized their fixed, regular, and ordered qualities. The frequency with which Roman writers spoke in those sorts of terms about the diverse natures of things has been brought out with particular clarity in the work of Daryn Lehoux, who has highlighted the ease with which Latin texts characterized nature in 'lawlike' terms.[87] They might do so by making exactly the same metaphorical analogy between natural behaviours and prescribed laws that we now do, as for instance Pliny's *Naturalis historia* ('Natural History') did when it appealed to a 'law of nature' (*lex naturae*) to explain the observable and regular movements of the winds.[88] In other instances, their mode of expression might less exactly mirror our own, turning instead on the language of agreements and contracts rather than laws and decrees; but it remained coupled with the same basic sense that order and regularity could be discerned in a wide range of natural phenomena. These Roman views of the world still lay close at hand in the early Middle Ages, as scribes from England and elsewhere produced new

---

[85] Daston, *Rules*, p. 229. [86] Daston, *Rules*, p. 225. [87] Lehoux, 'Laws of nature'.
[88] Pliny, *Naturalis historia*, II.45 (ed. Rackham, vol. I, p. 258); Lehoux, 'Laws of nature', p. 537.

manuscript copies of ancient texts, and as translators turned to the vernacular to give new life to older Latin images of natural order.[89] Where the late antique philosopher Boethius (d. 524) had once sought to capture the unchanging movements of the stars by imagining them abiding by the terms of an 'ancient peace', drawn up according to 'the laws (*iura*) of the lofty Thunderer', so in turn did an Old English translation of Boethius's work still find it comprehensible to talk about the stars 'keeping the old peace in which they were created'.[90] If, as Lehoux argues, 'it is abundantly clear that nature is being conceived of as lawlike quite commonly in Latin sources', then it is equally clear that those same conceptions remained available – and intelligible – to early medieval thinkers in England and beyond.[91]

Early medieval English writers not only endorsed ancient ideas about the fixed order of the world but also willingly expanded on them. The Old English translation of Boethius's *De consolatione Philosophiae* ('On the Consolation of Philosophy') offers several indications of where an educated early medieval mind might go when given the opportunity to reflect on the ordered nature of the universe. The identity of the person to whom that mind belonged remains debated. The translation begins with the statement that 'King Alfred was the translator of this book', but the trustworthiness of that attribution to the ninth-century king of Wessex remains debated.[92] Linguistic considerations certainly place the translator in the late ninth or early tenth century, but further consensus beyond the date has not yet been reached.[93] Whoever he was, the translator frequently found himself prompted by his Latin source to convey his own convictions about the world as he understood it, and it is in that respect that his vernacular adaptation of Boethius can assist us here.

Seeking to capture the regular operation of the universe in a single image, the translator of the Old English Boethius asked his readers to think of the movement of a cartwheel. 'Just as the wheels turn around the axle of a cart while the axle remains still', the translator said, so too does 'the whole of the moving and

---

[89] For an early English copy of Pliny's *Naturalis historia*, which is now incomplete but which looks originally to have included, for instance, the parts of book II in which Pliny had discussed the 'law of nature' governing the winds, see Garrison, 'Insular copy'.

[90] Boethius, *De consolatione Philosophiae*, IV, metre 6 (ed. Bieler, p. 84); *Old English Boethius* (B-text), ch. 39 (ed. Godden and Irvine, vol. I, p. 368). In what follows, all references to the Old English text are to the original prose translation of Boethius (the B-text), rather than to the later prosimetrical adaptation (the C-text). On the relationship of the two versions, see Godden and Irvine, *Old English Boethius*, vol. I, pp. 44–6.

[91] Lehoux, 'Laws of nature', p. 538.

[92] *Old English Boethius*, preface (ed. Godden and Irvine, vol. I, p. 239). For the key areas of debate, compare Godden, 'Did King Alfred write anything?'; and Bately, 'Did King Alfred actually translate anything?'.

[93] Godden and Irvine, *Old English Boethius*, vol. I, pp. 145–6.

turning creation turn around the still, stable and single God, and he controls all creatures in the manner that he had intended at the Beginning and has continued to do ever since'.[94] The image was the translator's own addition to the ideas which Boethius had been expressing in this part of his text.[95] It conveyed the translator's sense that the world, like the wheel, was continually in motion, and that its movements were regular and predictable. Its course had not changed since God had first set it moving, and every created thing therefore found itself 'turned again to the same course that it ran before, so that it comes again to be renewed'.[96] These motions were sometimes plain to see: they 'move the firmament and the stars', the translator reminded his readers.[97] But if it was true that 'every created thing turns on itself like a wheel', as the translator argued, then these same motions extended far beyond the outwardly visible, down into the basic building-blocks of the universe.[98] The turn of the wheel must surely also 'control the four elements, namely water, earth, fire, and air. God regulates and fashions them, sometimes unfashioning them again and bringing them forth in a different form'.[99] Deep within the inner natures of all things, the same endless motions which governed the rest of the universe played on at a scale that had to be grasped by the intellect rather than by direct observation. 'There is fire in the stones and in the water', readers of the Old English Boethius were told, 'very difficult to see, but it is in there all the same'.[100] Even when human sight proved insufficient to look directly into the deepest parts of God's Creation, Boethius's Old English translator saw no reason to believe that fixed, regular, and predictable behaviours would not also operate in the most inscrutable parts of the physical universe.

Just how far a person might go in pursuit of the hidden regularities which ran through the world was a matter of individual judgement, and it is clear that some early medieval English men and women were prepared to credit the existence of phenomena that went significantly beyond even the Old English Boethius's frames of reference. Just as the turn of the seasons made it possible to know when fruit would appear on the trees or crops ripen in the fields, perhaps one could also become cognisant of other sorts of temporal patterns too, and begin to see a hidden order within ostensibly random events. Perhaps merchants ought to pay attention to the waxing of the moon, in case its age

---

[94] *Old English Boethius*, ch. 39 (ed. Godden and Irvine, vol. I, p. 363).
[95] See Godden and Irvine, *Old English Boethius*, vol. II, pp. 466–7.
[96] *Old English Boethius*, ch. 21 (ed. Godden and Irvine, vol. I, p. 285).
[97] *Old English Boethius*, ch. 39 (ed. Godden and Irvine, vol. I, p. 364); cf. Boethius, *De consolatione Philosophiae*, IV, prose 6 (ed. Bieler, p. 80).
[98] *Old English Boethius*, ch. 25 (ed. Godden and Irvine, vol. I, p. 294).
[99] *Old English Boethius*, ch. 39 (ed. Godden and Irvine, vol. I, p. 364).
[100] *Old English Boethius*, ch. 33 (ed. Godden and Irvine, vol. I, p. 317).

had any bearing on the success of their enterprise. Perhaps famines could be predicted in advance by listening out for thunderstorms in the hours of the night. Perhaps the character of a child bore some relation to the day of the week on which they were born. Assurances on each of those points, and on a great many other such matters, could be found scattered across a wide variety of ancient texts, to which intellectuals in early medieval England not only had access, but sometimes clearly devoted serious efforts in searching out. The three examples which I have just given – of happenings potentially tied to times of day, days of the week, and phases of the moon – are all contained within a single mid-eleventh-century manuscript (London, British Library, Cotton Tiberius A.iii) which exhibits a particularly developed interest in obtaining, gathering together, and making newly accessible texts of this kind (Figure 6).[101] It is customary to refer to these miscellaneous works as 'prognostic texts', on the basis that they sought to equip their users with information about things yet to come. Births, deaths, prosperity, calamity, the state of the weather, the prospects of the sick, and success or failure in various enterprises were all revealed by prognostic texts to adhere to regular and predictable patterns. Those patterns could be learned, and future events thereby anticipated in advance, through attentiveness to a wide range of signs, including dreams, weather events, celestial phenomena, and the calendar. A few more of the examples which the compiler of Cotton Tiberius A.iii included in his collection can help to indicate the varied kinds of outcomes and significations that prognostic texts might base themselves around:

> 'If the moon is new on a Friday, then there will be good hunting in that month'.[102]
>
> 'If someone dreams that they kiss a dead person, then a long and happy life lies ahead for them'.[103]
>
> 'If it thunders from the east during the tenth hour of the day, it signifies the fall of cities'.[104]

Not only were the techniques and applications of prognostic texts multiple and various, but so too were the types of people who might be prepared to give them credence. Learned ecclesiastics found room for them in compilations of religious and devotional material, as did scribes producing books of medicinal remedies for practical use, and occasional references to them in

---

[101] The entire collection of prognostic texts in this manuscript are ed. and trans. Liuzza, *Prognostics*, with the examples mentioned here at pp. 172 (thunder signifying scarcity), 190 (merchants and the moon), and 218 (childbirth and the days of the week).
[102] Ed. Liuzza, *Prognostics*, p. 198.   [103] Ed. Liuzza, *Prognostics*, p. 208.
[104] Ed. Liuzza, *Prognostics*, p. 172.

vernacular sermons speak to their potential appeal to a broader cross-section of early medieval English society.[105]

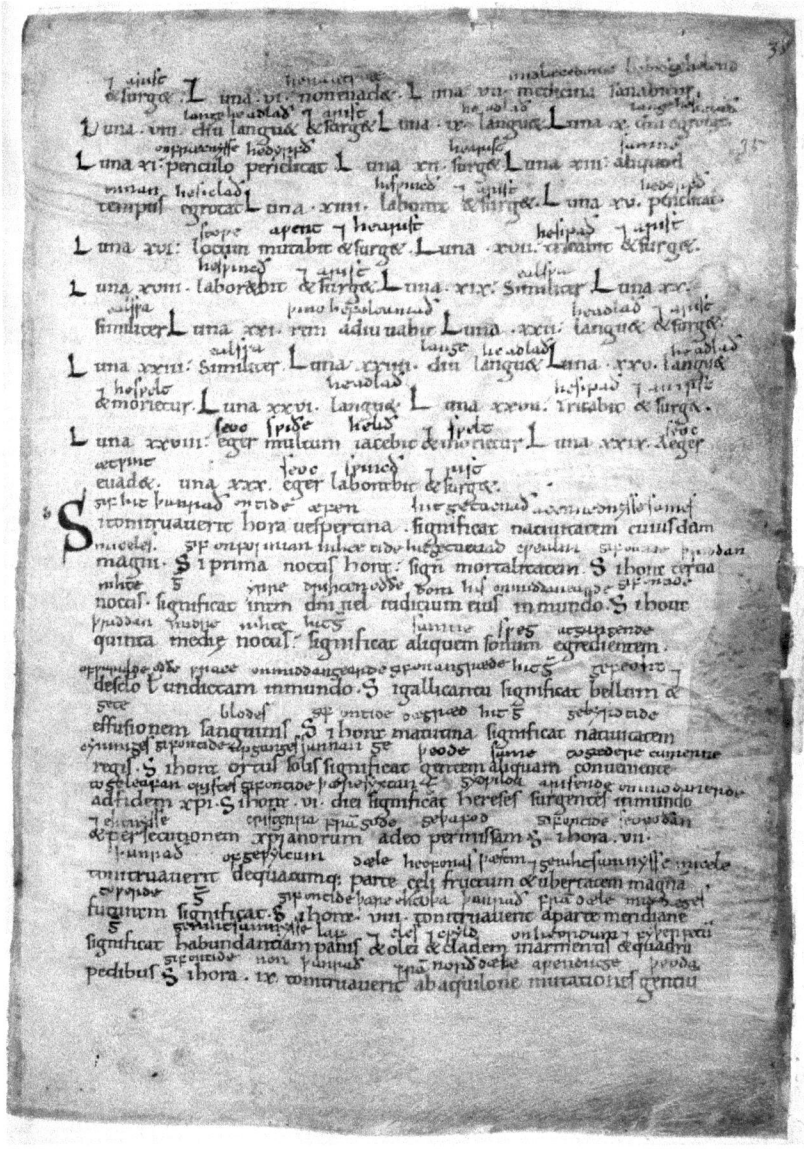

Figure 6 Prognostication by thunder and the moon, in a manuscript produced at the cathedral priory of Christ Church, Canterbury (London, British Library, Cotton Tiberius A.iii, fol. 37r). By permission of the British Library.

---

[105] Useful surveys of these practices and their circulation are Chardonnens, *Prognostics*; Liuzza, *Prognostics*; and Heiduk, Herbers, and Lehner (eds.), *Prognostication*.

Prognostic texts were typically unambiguous about the things that they purported to foretell, and about the techniques which were to be employed in order to reveal those future happenings. They posed greater difficulties, however, to anyone seeking to categorize the *kind* of knowledge which was contained within them. Were these the sorts of ideas which homilists warned their congregations against, informing them as Ælfric did that 'anyone who puts their faith in sorcerous divinations . . . is no Christian, but a wicked apostate'?[106] Or were they instead basically the same as the sorts of claims made by respected authorities like Bede, about the way that one could foretell changes in the weather up to a month ahead, by looking for signs in the appearance of the moon, the colour of the sky, or the behaviour of animals?[107] Those with access to prognostic texts were clearly alive to the problem and recognized the ease with which individuals might disagree about how and where to distinguish the licit from the illicit. At some point before the mid-eleventh century, for instance, a list of 'evil days' was translated from Latin into Old English by someone who was clearly willing to credit its central claim that there were certain days of the year on which it was harmful to undertake particular activities, most especially to undergo medical treatment.[108] The translation sought to make this useful information available to a wider readership and identified the days which were therefore to be avoided: two in each calendar month, plus certain days in the lunar cycle, and also the feast of All Saints' Day. Despite the translator's evident willingness to accept the authority of his source, he clearly anticipated the likelihood that others might not share that view. He addressed the possibility of scepticism head on, in short additional remarks offered to his readers here and there as he adapted his source. 'This is no sorcery', he informed his readers in one such addition, 'but only what wise men have discovered through holy wisdom, just as God directed them'. In the Introduction to this Element, we heard Ælfric making distinctions of a very similar kind between what was and was not to be understood as 'sorcery' (*wiglung*), and it is not wholly inconceivable that this short treatise should also be counted among his works. It certainly exhibits several connections with his known writings, but scholars have disagreed as to whether these ought to be taken as evidence of authorship, or only of influence.[109] Less important for us than the identity of the

---

[106] Ælfric, *Lives of the Saints*, XVI.2 (ed. Clayton and Mullins, vol. II, p. 124). For similar opinions in earlier texts, some of which may have informed Ælfric's sermon, see Meaney, 'Sources', pp. 480–1.

[107] Bede, *De natura rerum*, ch. 36 (ed. Jones, pp. 222–3), drawing upon Isidore, *De natura rerum*, ch. 38 (ed. Fontaine, pp. 299–303).

[108] Old English text: Chardonnens, *Prognostics*, pp. 370–2; Latin source: Chardonnens, 'Ælfric', pp. 150–1.

[109] Compare Chardonnens, 'Ælfric'; and Shaw, 'Just as the books tell us'.

translator, however, is the manner in which he sought to justify his belief in the purported 'evil days' by means of a striking appeal to empirical proof. There had once been a doctor, the translator said, 'who knew all this [and who] let blood from his horse at the stated time – and soon it lay dead'.[110]

We should reserve judgement about the likelihood that an early medieval doctor really had once conducted a test upon his unfortunate horse in order to prove the reality of the supposedly 'evil days', in the way that this Old English treatise alleged. The truthfulness of the story is less significant than the fact that our Old English author evidently felt that potential objectors might find it persuasive. The notion that one *could* conceivably test the veracity of other people's claims about the world was clearly not unthinkable in this period. The capacity of the natural world to confound expectations was readily acknowledged, for example, by the compilers of medical books, as they catalogued the varied and sometimes surprising properties of a range of organic and inorganic materials. They prepared their readers to see first-hand that certain plants, for instance, contained within them 'so great a power as you would never have thought they could have'.[111] These properties could be learned, and then deployed in the service of a wide range of human needs, when one knew which stones offered protection against lightning (jet), which berries produced a juice that improved one's hearing (elderberries), or which animals possessed internal organs that could relieve pain after childbirth (hares).[112] Running through all this was the tacit promise of replicability. However it was that these properties had first been discovered, they could be depended upon to manifest themselves identically for every new person who sought to make use of them.

The fact that the things of the physical world could be put to such varied and abundant uses was typically understood in fundamentally anthropocentric terms during this period. The view expressed by Bede, in a commentary on the book of Genesis, that it was 'for man himself that all things on earth were made' had occurred to others too, in England and beyond, for centuries.[113] Late Roman physicians like Theodorus Priscianus had already taken up the basic theme in the fourth century, confident from their professional experience that 'the great powers of seeds, fruits, herbs, and everything else' must all have been 'produced for human beings'; and recent work by Meg Leja has drawn attention to

---

[110] Chardonnens, *Prognostics*, pp. 370–2.
[111] *Old English Herbarium*, ch. 12.4 (ed. D'Aronco, p. 90); cf. pseudo-Apuleius, *Herbarius*, ch. 11.4 (ed. Howald and Sigerist, p. 44).
[112] Jet: *Bald's Leechbook*, II.66 (ed. Cockayne, vol. II, pp. 296–8); and see Kitson, 'Lapidary traditions: part I'. Elderberries: *Bald's Leechbook*, I.3.9 (ed. Cockayne, vol. II, p. 42). Hares: *Medicina de quadrupedibus*, ch. 5.6 (ed. D'Aronco, p. 386); translating Sextus Placitus, *Liber medicinae ex animalibus* (A-text), ch. 3.6 (ed. Howald and Sigerist, p. 242).
[113] Bede, *In Genesim*, I.i.11–13 (ed. Jones, pp. 14–15).

the particularly emphatic way that intellectuals in the Carolingian Empire expressed similar ideas for themselves, certain that 'all the beautiful things of the world which God created for human beings to use' indicated the depth of God's love for humanity.[114]

These underlying convictions could nevertheless be taken in one of two different directions, as late antique and early medieval thinkers considered the world around them. The first was to take abundance and diversity in the natural world as indications of the ease with which human beings could turn it to their needs. That had been Theodorus Priscianus's point when he had spoken about the 'great powers' of so many natural substances, all of which lay close to hand in such great quantities that any person, at any moment, could swiftly obtain what they needed. As a physician, it was medical need that was foremost in his mind, and he spoke with exasperation about the woeful slowness with which so many of his fellow professionals worked. Nothing could be more straightforward than searching out the raw materials with which to make medicines, Theodorus said, because 'Nature has placed medicine even in the lowliest of plants, so that no-one in any place or at any time will be left without the service of healing'.[115]

It seems likely that Theodorus's opinion could have been shared by some of the medical specialists of early medieval England too, as we will shortly see. But before we return to the English sources, we need also to recognize that there was also an alternative view, which saw in the richness of the natural world not simplicity, but unavoidable complexity. The innate properties of natural resources were *so* abundant and *so* diverse that they could easily lead to bewilderment, for although one could be confident that they did indeed hold the key to countless human needs, their myriad forms and properties could be dizzyingly difficult to navigate. This was the view expressed in passing in one of the vernacular sagas composed in early medieval Ireland, known as the *Cath Maige Tuired* ('The [Second] Battle of Mag Tuired'). It was a text devoted to the telling of mythic stories about the island's ancient past; and one of them revealed that the individual powers of plants and herbs had been known in those days to the Túatha Dé Danann, the ancient divinities of Ireland, who had briefly been able to harvest them 'according to their properties'. But soon after their discovery, the story continued, these plants had become 'mixed [up], so that no-one knows their proper healing qualities unless the Holy Spirit taught them afterwards'.[116] An appreciation of natural diversity runs through this brief

---

[114] Theodorus Priscianus, *Euporiston*, I.1 (ed. Rose, p. 3); Leja, 'Sacred art' (with discussion of the quoted passage at pp. 20–1).
[115] Theodorus Priscianus, *Euporiston*, I.1 (ed. Rose, p. 4).
[116] *Cath Maige Tuired*, ch. 35 (ed. and trans. Gray, pp. 32–3). On the Túatha Dé Danann, see now Williams, *Ireland's Immortals* (with discussion of *Cath Maige Tuired* on pp. 92–127).

story, no less strongly than through Theodorus Priscianus's discussion of the same theme – but the saga-writer's concluding remark about the disordered and unintuitive state of the natural world expresses a wholly different view of what that meant for men and women who might wish to turn it to human use. Although the properties of the natural world were certainly varied, readers of the *Cath Maige Tuired* were being expected to agree that those properties could also be hard to identify, confusing to navigate, and comprehensible only with otherworldly assistance.

The preceding examples have taken us some distance from early medieval England, but provide us with ways of thinking about human recourse to the varied properties of natural resources, which we can profitably consider in relation to English sources which touch on similar themes. Contained within the Old English medical books are a number of remedies that are certainly capable of supporting the sort of views which Theodorus Priscianus had held, about the straightforward intelligibility of natural properties and their uses. England was unusual in this period in having produced a large body of medical writing in the vernacular, surviving now in several different collections – each quite different in character to the next – which together attest to a rich store of pharmacological learning, built up over many centuries.[117] The collection which we know as *Bald's Leechbook* (on the basis of the colophon which names an otherwise unknown Bald as the person who 'has this book') are several remedies which promise that certain ailments could be cured by the application of ingredients that exhibited some kind of connection with the nature of the illness being treated. The bladders of certain animals, for instance, prove in *Bald's Leechbook* to be efficacious in treating urinary incontinence, trusting it would seem in an easily appreciated connection between the afflicted part of the human sufferer and the corresponding organ obtained from another healthy creature.[118] Similarities could be found in the behaviours of plants too, as another remedy in the same collection indicated when it said that bald men could make use of willow leaves in order to encourage their hair to regrow, presumably inspired by the vigour with which willow trees produce new shoots after being cut back.[119]

Other remedies in the Old English medical books, however, were much more likely to lead to the conclusion that the properties of the natural world could be maddeningly counter-intuitive, in just the way that the *Cath Maige Tuired* had suggested. Some treatments depended on complex combinations of different materials, gathered in particular ways and brought together according to precise

---

[117] For wide surveys, see Cameron, *Anglo-Saxon Medicine*; and Kesling, *Medical Texts*.
[118] *Bald's Leechbook*, I.37 (ed. Cockayne, vol. II, pp. 88–90).
[119] *Bald's Leechbook*, I.87.2 (ed. Cockayne, vol. II, p. 156); Storms, *Anglo-Saxon Magic*, p. 58.

instructions. The bark of trees provided relief for 'a worm-eaten and pestilential body', according to *Bald's Leechbook* – but only when taken in equal amounts from three different kinds of tree (oak, ash, and elder), some of which had to be collected from specific parts of the tree (the lowest part of the north-facing side, in the case of the elder), and then mixed together with the roots of another two plants (elecampane and dock) and seven other ingredients (including acorn meal, horse fat, and ship's tar).[120] Even much simpler instructions, like the *Leechbook*'s recommendation to use butter to counteract poison, might turn out to require exceptional care in sourcing one's ingredients: butter intended for this purpose had to be churned only on a Friday, from milk taken only from 'a cow or hind of a single colour', if it was to have any benefit to the sufferer.[121]

Anyone who intended to make use of these sorts of remedies must have been grateful that they possessed written instructions to help them navigate the complex resources of the natural world, but may also have wondered justifiably about how these remedies had ever been devised in the first place. We have already heard the view expressed in the *Cath Maige Tuired* that no-one would ever be able to 'know the proper healing qualities' of herbs and plants 'unless the Holy Spirit taught them'. The occasional appearance in Old English medical writings of remedies attributed to specific named individuals – in notes which observe that 'Oxa taught this remedy', or that this was 'a remedy that Dun taught' – do certainly indicate that the healing properties of natural resources were not always self-evident, being known at first only by a few especially knowledgeable people.[122] Exactly how the likes of Oxa or Dun had themselves become aware of these little-known facts of the natural world, the remedy-books gave no indication. Human ingenuity was always a perfectly plausible explanation; but there was also in this period nothing outlandish in the notion that human beings could have been instructed in such matters by otherworldly assistance. The pseudepigraphical book of 1 Enoch was not unknown in early medieval England, and included within it an account of the role that wayward angels had once played in teaching the first generations of human beings about the properties of plants, metals, and other secrets of the created world.[123] Readers of English saints' Lives could find stories about much more recent events which confirmed that suprahuman beings might continue to instruct people about matters of this kind, as the Northumbrian saint Cuthbert (d. 687) had discovered when an angel came to him one day with recommendations

---

[120] *Bald's Leechbook*, I.54 (ed. Cockayne, vol. II, p. 127).
[121] *Bald's Leechbook*, I.45.5 (ed. Cockayne, vol. II, p. 112).
[122] On the attributions, see Banham, 'Dun'.
[123] 1 Enoch 7:1 and 8:1–3 (trans. Black, pp. 28–9). For knowledge of the text in England, see the relevant entries in Biggs (ed.), *Apocrypha*, pp. 8–10.

about the ingredients and methods with which to prepare a poultice for his injured knee.[124] Early medieval English men and women knew that human beings were adept at acting on the knowledge which they possessed about the various properties of natural substances, and were confident in that regard that the abundant resources of the natural world could be turned to a multitude of human uses. Even so, there evidently remained something enticing about the possibility that there was still more that could be known, already understood by otherworldly intelligences and perhaps one day to be added to the store of human wisdom as well.

Although it was clearly valuable to gain knowledge about the natures of things, early medieval English men and women knew too that there were ways to bend natural properties into new forms, to make them behave differently or display different characteristics to those which they would otherwise 'naturally' possess. Shoots cut from one plant could be grafted onto the rootstocks of others, in a practice that the apostle Paul had once described as 'contrary to nature' (*contra naturam*) but with which ancient and early medieval peoples were clearly familiar.[125] The intended outcome, as Cassiodorus (d. c. 585) had once concisely summarized it in the sixth century, was to ensure that trees which 'produce bitter and sterile fruits by themselves' would instead bear fruits that 'plump up with the sweetest fruitfulness'; and the practice was certainly well known in England by the time that an Old English treatise, from around the year 1000, mentioned it in a list of the spring-time duties of reeves.[126] The behaviours and dispositions of animals could be altered too, again with human utility in mind. Even the mightiest creatures 'can be tamed by human skill', Ælfric of Eynsham informed his congregation in one of his sermons. It was the example of the elephant that Ælfric had in mind on that occasion (and on several others, in what was clearly a subject of considerable interest for him), and he observed that these enormous and formidable creatures were in fact capable of being 'marvellously trained for battle'.[127] Elephants of course, as Ælfric observed, 'have never come into England'; but other species had been tamed and trained by English hands over many centuries. It was well understood that these endeavours were more likely to succeed when they sought to mould and develop the characteristics which creatures already possessed. When Æthelberht II, king of Kent (d. 762), hoped to acquire a pair of falcons from overseas with which to

---

[124] *Vita Cuthberti*, I.4 (ed. Colgrave, pp. 66–8); Bede, *Vita Cuthberti*, ch. 2 (ed. Colgrave, pp. 158–60).

[125] Romans 11:24.

[126] Cassiodorus, *Expositio psalmorum*, XCV.12 (ed. Adriaen, vol. II, p. 868). *Gerefa*, ch. 12, ed. Liebermann, *Gesetze*, vol. I, p. 454.

[127] Ælfric, *Lives of the Saints*, XXIII (ed. Clayton and Mullins, vol. II, pp. 316–18). See also Cross, 'Elephant'; Thornbury, 'Zoology'; and Christie, 'Idea'.

hunt cranes, for instance, he explained that he had been required to look abroad 'because there seem to be very few hawks of this kind to be found in our lands ... which produce young that are good enough to be reared, tamed and trained, and that are also agile yet fierce enough at heart for the stated purpose'.[128] Human interventions upon the behaviours of other creatures still necessitated, in other words, the careful scrutiny of natural characteristics and innate dispositions, even as they sought to produce from them new behaviours that would never otherwise have arisen of their own accord.

To some extent, therefore, natural characteristics could be modified. It was likely, however, that whatever changes resulted from them were at best temporary, and perhaps even only superficial. That was the view expressed emphatically in the Old English Boethius, through a series of images supplied by the text's Latin source but which prompted the Old English translator into his own rumination on the limited capacity of human beings to effect change upon the natures of other creatures. Boethius had made the point that all things possess an innate desire for their natural state, and had substantiated his claim first with the example of a captive lion breaking free from its chains after tasting blood, and then by considering the behaviour of a caged bird yearning for its old life in the woods (Figure 7).[129] When the Old English translator took

Figure 7 Lions with their prey, in the illustration to Psalm 103 from the Harley Psalter (London, British Library, Harley 603, fol. 51v). By permission of the British Library.

---

[128] *Die Briefe*, CV (ed. Tangl, p. 231).
[129] Boethius, *De consolatione Philosophiae*, III, metre 2 (ed. Bieler, pp. 40–1).

up these same examples, he turned them from images of captivity into images of domestication:

> For if the lion ever happens to taste blood – even though it may be very tame and have strong chains, and greatly love and also fear its master – it straight-away forgets its recent tameness and remembers the wild ways of its ancestors. Then it begins to roar and to break its chains, and bites first its trainer and then whatever it can catch, humans and animals alike. Woodland birds do similarly: no matter how well tamed they are, if they come into the woods, they reject their trainers and live in their natural state, even if their trainers offer them the same foods to which they had grown accustomed while tame. If they can enjoy the woods then they no longer care for those foods, and instead think it better for them that the forest resounds for them, and that they hear the call of other birds.[130]

The repeated mentions of 'tameness' here were the Old English translator's addition to Boethius's imagery; and having inserted them, the translator immediately observed that neither tameness nor even 'great love' towards a human master would ultimately prevent these creatures from wishing at last to 'live in their natural state' (*wuniað on heora gecynde*). Although Boethius's central point remained unchanged in the Old English adaptation, the translator's unforced yet insistent emphasis on the unalterable natures of even the most 'well tamed' of creatures invited Old English readers to consider the additional question of how deeply, if at all, human beings could ever hope to effect true change upon the natures of other beings.

At the same time, however, early medieval English Christians were regularly told that there were many things in the world around them which had indeed been irrevocably changed from their natural course, and which bore constant witness to the existence and the might of otherworldly powers. There was said, for instance, to be a valley in the English midlands where the grass was never depleted in any way by any grazing animal, but sprang back ever more vigorously every time that it was cropped, and which exerted such a mysterious attraction upon cows from the nearby hillsides that they would independently seek it out, before returning home with udders full enough to produce more milk than an entire herd. The reason that plants and animals in this particular valley had begun to act in this otherwise inconceivable way was that there lay in that valley the undiscovered tomb of a saint.[131] The story joined countless other such reports about the marvels with which God made known and glorified his chosen saints, in circumstances which differed markedly from one to the next but which frequently centred upon events in which the fixed properties and behaviours of things suddenly no longer followed

---

[130] *Old English Boethius*, ch. 25 (ed. Godden and Irvine, vol. I, pp. 293–4).
[131] *Vita Kenelmi*, ch. 9 (ed. Love, p. 62).

their regular patterns. If God so chose, it was 'not difficult for [him] to decree that ravenous decay should not devour the corpses placed under the earth', and hagiographers who marvelled to find that the bodies and garments of the saints might remain unaffected by decay after years in the tomb expressed their expectation that those same relics were not only 'uncorrupted' (*incorruptus*) but truly also now 'incorruptible' (*incorruptibilis*).[132] They sometimes said outright that the phenomena which they described had taken place 'contrary to nature' (*contra naturam*), as a Northumbrian hagiographer named Stephen did in the course of story about a group of arsonists who had found that their fire was *extinguished*, rather than spread, by the thatch of the building that they were attempting to raze.[133] In truth, however, readers will scarcely have needed a hagiographer to guide them to that conclusion when they encountered stories about strips of cloth which ran with blood when cut by a knife, walking-staffs which sprouted roots and leaves when thrust into the earth, or lifeless children returned from death at the touch of a hand – all of which were enthusiastically reported in English saints' Lives written between the eighth century and the eleventh.[134]

Such stories gained their power precisely because they attested to events which manifestly ran counter not just to what was *normal*, but also what was otherwise known to be *possible* in a world which otherwise dependably adhered to the fixed, stable and predictable rules with which it had been constituted. Early medieval hagiographers would, I suspect, have found themselves in fundamental agreement with Durkheim when he argued that 'In order to arrive at the idea of the supernatural, it is not enough ... to be witnesses to unexpected events; it is also necessary that these be conceived as impossible, that is to say, irreconcilable with an order which, rightly or wrongly, appears to us to be implied in the nature of things'.[135] Early medieval writings attest both to the strong sentiment of their authors and audiences that order could be found 'in the nature of things', and to their equally strong conviction in an 'idea of the supernatural' which not only ran through that natural order, but which could sometimes also reshape it.

3 Acts and Expectations

If English hagiographers were correct to say that the natures of earthly things presented not the slightest impediment to divine power, then it is little wonder that their contemporaries might sometimes be prepared to take extraordinary steps in

---

[132] Bede, *Vita Cuthberti*, chs. 42–3 and 45 (ed. Colgrave, pp. 292–6 and 298).
[133] Stephen, *Vita Wilfridi*, ch. 67 (ed. Colgrave, p. 144).
[134] Bleeding cloth: *Liber beatae Gregorii*, ch. 21 (ed. Colgrave, pp. 108–10). Growing staffs: *Vita Kenelmi*, ch. 6 (ed. Love, p. 58). Resurrected children: Stephen, *Vita Wilfridi*, ch. 18 (ed. Colgrave, pp. 38–40).
[135] Durkheim, trans. Swain, *Elementary Forms*, p. 28.

the hope that they might benefit from its assistance. In the summer of 1009, prompted by news of an immense Danish army recently arrived in England, it was the leading men of the kingdom who found themselves considering the form that those steps might take. The result of their deliberations was an extensive programme of ritual action in which every adult person in the kingdom was meant to participate, 'so that we may obtain God's mercy and grace'. It involved the organization of barefoot processions, periods of fasting, collective and individual prayer, and assiduous acts of charity and alms-giving, all which together would, it was hoped, ensure 'that almighty God might show mercy upon us and grant us victory over our enemies, and peace'.[136] The scale of what was being envisioned was certainly remarkable, and instructions for how it was all to be carried out were promulgated by the king, Æthelred II (d. 1016), and his councillors at a meeting held at Bath shortly after the Danish army had landed. The constituent parts of this national programme of devotion belonged, however, to a well-established repertoire of rites and rituals that had been deeply familiar to generations of early medieval Christians, in England and elsewhere, for centuries.[137] For Wulfstan of York (d. 1023), the archbishop who had drafted Æthelred's proclamation, it was a certainty that 'great and celebrated' things regularly resulted when the age-old rites of the Church were performed correctly.[138] If he and his contemporaries were to 'entreat God intently so that we may obtain his mercy and grace' in supporting them against crises and calamities that they could not hope to withstand on their own, they might at least take comfort from the fact that the proper means of securing that otherworldly assistance were already at their disposal.[139]

The specific situation for which Æthelred and his advisors had devised their programme of national prayer and penitence was very far from being the only occasion on which early medieval English men and women might be found giving serious thought to the possibility of divine intervention. Archbishop Wulfstan himself thought that it should be immediately sought any time that 'profound misfortune falls upon the nation', and he soon produced a revised version of the ordinances of 1009 which he hoped would enable his contemporaries to seek God's assistance against 'soldiers or starvation, burning or bloodshed, bad harvest or bad weather, [and] pestilence among animals or among humans'.[140] The wide range of other, more personal misfortunes which might encourage someone to appeal to the heavens was well known to the writers and

---

[136] *VII Æthelred*, ch. 7.1, ed. Liebermann, *Gesetze*, vol. I, pp. 260–1. I quote from the Latin version of the text which Keynes ('Abbot', p. 180) judges to be 'closest to the programme of prayer as authorized by the king and his councillors at Bath'.

[137] See Keynes, 'Abbot', pp. 181–9.   [138] Wulfstan, *Polity* (ed. Jost, p. 104).

[139] *VII Æthelred*, ch. 7.1, ed. Liebermann, *Gesetze*, vol. I, p. 261.

[140] Two adaptations of *VII Æthelred* which have been revised in this way are printed by Napier, *Wulfstan*, pp. 169–75 [nos. XXXV and XXXVI]. Of these, it is Napier XXXV which seems

readers of hagiography, in which the individual circumstances of the needy and the desperate served to demonstrate the endless benevolence of God and the holy saints through whom he worked. Hagiographers told stories about blind men abandoned on the road by their sighted companions, enslaved women facing unjust punishment from cruel masters, and the 'innumerable multitude' of people driven to despair by ill health.[141] They described how each in turn had experienced a miraculous reversal of fortune after turning to the divine, and asked their readers to contemplate what it might mean that God was 'showing the world so many and such unheard-of marvels in recent times'.[142]

The acts required of men and women who hoped to obtain otherworldly assistance in such matters could sometimes be extremely simple, requiring nothing more than the utterance of a single prayer or the gift of a single object.[143] But they could also attain remarkable complexity, taking place over an extended period of time as we have seen King Æthelred demanding of his subjects, or requiring the successful completion of an intricate series of actions and invocations. Just how intricate they might become is illustrated especially vividly by one Old English account of a procedure which could be deployed by communities whose crops had begun to grow less plentifully in their fields, and which has come to be known as the *æcerbot* or 'field-remedy' (Figure 8).[144] The land itself was first to be prepared by removing sods of earth under cover of darkness, and by collecting cuttings from the trees and plants which grew upon it (avoiding hardwood trees and burdock). Every animal which grazed there was also to be milked, and the milk mixed with the cuttings and with oil, honey, yeast, and holy water. That mixture in turn should then be dripped upon the gathered sods of earth, accompanied by the saying of prayers, benedictions, and biblical readings. The sods were then to be taken into a church for a priest to say four masses over them, then taken back out to the field and returned to their former locations, with wooden crosses inscribed with the names of the four evangelists buried underneath them. Prayers, blessings, and other invocations followed, some accompanied by movements and gestures that took account of the cardinal directions and the course of the sun. Still more remained to be done even now, as seeds were to be exchanged with beggars, ploughing equipment to be prepared with incense, fennel, and consecrated soap and salt, and a specially baked loaf to be laid in the first furrow cut by the plough, all accompanied by further prayers and recitations as directed.

---

likely in the main to be the work of Wulfstan, while stylistic and other considerations argue against his involvement in the production of Napier XXXVI: see Lionarons, *Homiletic Writings*, pp. 30–2.

[141] Lantfred, *Translatio*, chs. 4, 6, and 18 (ed. Lapidge, pp. 286, 288, and 300).
[142] Lantfred, *Translatio*, ch. 10 (ed. Lapidge, p. 294).
[143] Lantfred, *Translatio*, chs. 27 and 32 (ed. Lapidge, pp. 314 and 320–2).
[144] The text is edited in Storms, *Anglo-Saxon Magic*, pp. 172–6.

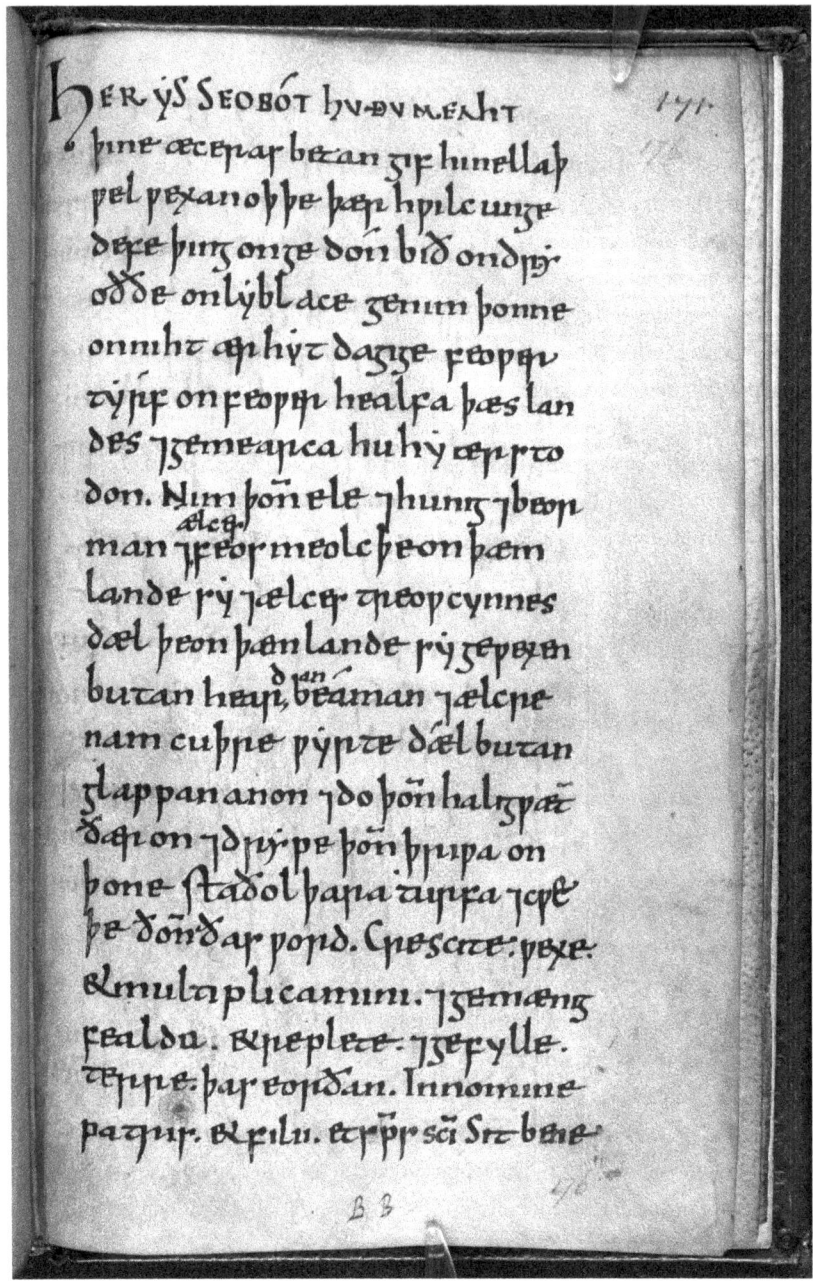

Figure 8 The beginning of the *æcerbot*: a 'remedy for how you can improve your fields if they will not grow properly, or if any harmful thing has been done by a sorcerer or by witchcraft' (London, British Library, Cotton Caligula, A.vii, fol. 176r). By permission of the British Library.

These were rites which had been devised as carefully as those by which King Æthelred had hoped to secure his kingdom against the threat of invasion. Their complex collection of physical gestures and spoken words attended both to the realities of agricultural practice (for instance, in their deliberate exclusion of certain trees and plants from the rite, so as not to promote growth in species which could prove undesirable on open ploughland), and to symbolic associations rooted in biblical imagery and other sources of inspiration (seen, for instance, in the instructions to combine milk, oil, honey, and yeast as a tangible echo of the 'four sacred liquids' of early medieval exegetical tradition).[145] At their core, however, even elaborate rituals like the *æcerbot* adhered to the same uncomplicated conviction that one could find in any simple prayer – that human beings regularly experienced difficulties and challenges, but could hope to gain assistance against them from a higher power that attended closely to their words and deeds.

Poor harvests, ill health, military threats, and other predicaments could of course be answered by a range of perfectly mundane human endeavours – by diligent labour in the fields, by the careful preparation of medicines, by the usual raising and supply of armed men, and so on. We should not think, therefore, that early medieval men and women turned to the supernatural in times of need because they had no other choice. Nor was it true that a person who sought supernatural support for their endeavours must therefore have wholly rejected the mundane. A farmer whose fields had been blessed to ensure their continued fertility would presumably still have thought it his business to see that they were manured, just as the sick might find it prudent to persevere with the services of human doctors at the same time as they made their misfortune known to God through prayer. But health and harvest were fragile endeavours, for which contemporaries freely admitted that no amount of technical expertise could entirely eliminate the possibility of failure.[146] Early medieval Christians could envisage several sorts of ways in which mundane actions and supernatural interventions might intersect, rather than compete, with one another. Perhaps divine power generally served to 'multiply' whatever was already there, as liturgical rites for the blessing of fields and new fruits frequently called upon God to do, and so could be understood to work symbiotically with whatever other practical steps had already been taken.[147] Or perhaps when one worked with materials and techniques which were easily compromised or otherwise

---

[145] Trees and plants to be avoided: Niles, '*Æcerbot* ritual', p. 50. Symbolism: Hill, '*Æcerbot* charm'.

[146] Healing: Sowerby, 'When medicine doesn't work'. Agriculture: Banham and Faith, *Farms and Farming*, p. 73.

[147] On the development of these rites and their circulation in England, see Rowe, 'Blessings for nature', pp. 182–245.

performed inconsistently, as some early medieval medical writers admitted about their art, then it must have seemed valuable to ensure that God himself had already looked favourably upon the intended outcome.[148] Something of that kind certainly seems to have been intended by whoever first recommended the singing of prayers into medicinal drinks, with 'the person's breath fully upon the liquid while they sing it', in the manner advised by one of the Old English remedy-books.[149] Although it sometimes suited hagiographers to list all the painful and unsuccessful medical treatments which the sick had pursued before they came eventually to the shrines of the saints, which at last delivered a cure that no human art had managed to achieve, our sources do not generally suggest that individuals were faced with a stark choice between whether to pursue natural or supernatural methods of achieving particular goals.[150] More often, they suggest that it was common to regard the natural and the supernatural operating in distinct yet complementary ways, which could both be harnessed in pursuit of the same goals.

As many of my preceding examples will already have indicated, human speech was often fundamental in efforts to harness the supernatural. It was nevertheless true that some kinds of speech acts were regarded more favourably than others. A frequent theme in sermons and in legislative writing during this period was that Christians should be careful to call upon the divine only through the acceptable channels of true prayer, and to guard themselves against other sorts of ritual speaking which were at best superstitious, and perhaps even sinful. Ecclesiastics who took up this theme tended to present it as if the distinction were clear-cut and unambiguous, by merely instructing their contemporaries to perform 'no charm but only the Lord's Prayer, the Creed, or some prayer that pertains to God', in the words of one Old English penitential.[151] They often drew substantially on the writings of earlier authorities on the subject: the passage from an Old English penitential from which I have just quoted, for instance, comes from a translation into Old English of a statement from the handbook compiled in an earlier century by Halitgar, bishop of Cambrai (d. 831), from sources which were already old when Halitgar brought them together.[152] To many it must have therefore seemed that the distinction between permissible and impermissible forms of ritual speaking was firm and well established.

---

[148] For unpredictability and medicine, see Sowerby, 'When medicine doesn't work'.
[149] *Lacnunga*, ch. 64 (ed. Niles, pp. 454–6).
[150] See, for example, Lantfred, *Translatio*, ch. 28 (ed. Lapidge, p. 316).
[151] *Old English Penitential*, II.23 (ed. Raith, p. 30).
[152] *Paenitentiale Halitgarii*, IV.26 (ed. Schmitz, vol. II, p. 285).

In practice, however, exactly how individuals drew the line between the acceptable and the unacceptable must often have been deeply subjective. Participants in the *æcerbot* ritual for the restoration of fields, for example, might have been struck by its array of Christian symbolism, by its requirement that some of the key actions had to be performed by a local priest upon his altar, and by its attentiveness to the associative connections between land, elements and scripture which had been established in mainstream biblical exegesis.[153] On the other hand, they might have found it just as striking that in the middle of the ceremony they were asked to make an address to 'the mother of earth', and may have wondered (as a long line of modern scholars have done since) who or what their words were directed towards.[154] The rites themselves gave no unambiguous answer to that question, and must therefore have remained open to divergent interpretation even among the people who participated in them.

One of the warnings which churchmen offered to their contemporaries in this period was that the acceptability of ritual actions could not be determined by the outcomes which resulted from them. It was a mistake, they argued, to suppose that anything which resulted in a positive or beneficial outcome was therefore self-evidently permissible. Forbidden acts might, of course, lead to harm and destruction (as indeed the *æcerbot* ritual itself demonstrates, since one of its intended functions was that it could be used 'if any harmful thing has been done by a sorcerer or by witchcraft').[155] But even practices which led to seemingly beneficial outcomes might still, in fact, operate according to illicit means. Augustine of Hippo had laid out the problem in the fifth century, by considering the different uses of plants in healing. It was entirely appropriate, he said, that sometimes a plant should be tied or applied to the body of a sick person, in such a way as to allow it to work 'by virtue of its own nature' (*ui naturae*). Sometimes, however, the force at work might not be that of the plant itself and its own innate properties, but rather of demons, for whom the affixing of the plant to the body represented a 'signifying bond' and an invitation for them to work their arts. This remained true, Augustine insisted, even if the sick person recovered their health as a result: 'the more it seems to work to good effect', he cautioned, 'the more therefore a Christian should rightly be cautious'.[156]

One early medieval reader who found Augustine's argument persuasive was Ælfric of Eynsham. He summarized Augustine's distinctions between the

---

[153] See Hill, '*Æcerbot* charm', pp. 215–19.
[154] For the range of suggested interpretations, some more persuasive than others, see Arthur, 'Heavenly field'.
[155] *Æcerbot*, lines 1–3, ed. Storms, *Anglo-Saxon Magic*, p. 172.
[156] Augustine, *De doctrina christiana*, II.29 (ed. Moreau, Bochet and Madec, pp. 204–6). For the significations established with demons, see also II.20 (p. 182); and Markus, 'Signs'.

permissible and the impermissible uses of plants affixed to the body in one of his own sermons, noting that 'the wise Augustine' had determined it to be 'forbidden sorcery if anyone binds a plant upon themselves, unless they are laying it upon a wound'.[157] The message was a simplified one, but Ælfric evidently understood the distinction which Augustine had been making. To bind herbs directly upon an open wound evidently represented for Ælfric a perfectly comprehensible way in which the substance of the plants could enter into the body of the injured person and contribute to their recovery ('by virtue of their own nature', as Augustine had put it). But he clearly knew that there were also other ways in which to affix materials to the human body, examples of which can certainly be found in Old English remedy-books – like the recommendation in one that certain plants could combat insanity if they were wrapped in cloth and hung around the neck, or the instruction in another that particular roots and seeds would enhance fertility if they were tied around the left thigh close to the genitals.[158] Perhaps such measures did indeed achieve their intended results, but both Augustine and Ælfric were evidently concerned about *how* precisely they might have done so, and therefore whether it was appropriate for Christians to make use of such arts.

I have so far refrained from using the word 'magic' in this discussion, but in truth it will already have been called to mind by the mentions made in our sources of 'forbidden sorcery', or by the harm that could be wreaked upon fields 'by a sorcerer or by witchcraft'. It was well known to early medieval men and women that some human beings could and did deploy 'magical arts' in pursuit of their goals (Figure 9). Even the bishop of Rome could be found in this period telling stories about the days when workers of evil magic (*malefici*) had been so numerous in the eternal city that some of them could be distinguished from the others in their command of magical practices (*in magicis operibus*).[159] Writers from England were still retelling these same stories in later centuries, identifying the deeds of the ancient magicians in Old English as their *drycræftas*; and they also offered new stories of their own about the things which the priests of the pre-Christian English kingdoms had once attempted to do 'by means of their magical arts' (*suis magicis artibus*, in the words of one Northumbrian hagiographer).[160] Such arts belonged not only to an ancient past but also to

---

[157] Ælfric, *Catholic Homilies*, I.31 (ed. Clemoes, p. 450). It is debateable whether Ælfric had a wider knowledge of *De doctrina christiana*, or whether he had encountered this passage via an intermediate source. The earliest English manuscript of the work postdates the Norman conquest (Salisbury, Cathedral Library, MS 106), and even Bede seems only to have known it through excerpts: see Ray, 'Who did Bede think he was?', p. 23.

[158] *Old English Herbarium*, ch. 58 (ed. D'Aronco, p. 162); *Leechbook III*, ch. 37 (ed. Cockayne, vol. II, pp. 328–30).

[159] Gregory the Great, *Dialogi*, I.4 (ed. de Vogüé, vol. II, pp. 38–42).

[160] *Old English Dialogues of Gregory the Great*, I.4 (ed. Hecht, vol. I, pp. 27–30). Stephen, *Vita Wilfridi*, ch. 13 (ed. Colgrave, p. 28).

Figure 9 An English depiction of the Egyptian magician Mambres, who 'opened the magical books of his brother Jamnes and revealed for himself the deep secrets of his brother's idolatry' (London, British Library, Cotton Tiberius B.v, fol. 87v). By permission of the British Library.

the here and now, and old biblical precepts about the impermissibility of deploying them still felt relevant to early medieval Christians. 'See that you pay no heed to magical acts (*ne gime drycræfta*)' ran one Old English rendering of a statement from the book of Deuteronomy, and the same sentiment was picked up by the compilers of lawcodes and penitentials who devised new measures against 'magic and incantation' (*drycræft and galdorcræft*) or against 'witches or sorcerers [or] enchanters' (*wiccan oððe wigeleras [oððe] scincræftcan*) wherever they still appeared.[161]

Early medieval English writers had no shortage of opinions about magic, and plenty of ways in both Latin and Old English to express them. In our own efforts to use 'magic' as a category of analysis, however, we face difficult choices about the degree to which our understanding of the word corresponds – or *should* correspond – to the understandings held by the writers of our sources. For Valerie Flint, in an influential study which sought to explore 'the rise of magic in early medieval Europe', it was sufficient to say that magic 'may be said to be the exercise of a preternatural control over nature by human beings, with the assistance of forces more powerful than they', and to proceed on the basis of

---

[161] *Old English Heptateuch*, Deut. 18:10 (ed. Marsden, p. 165); *Scriftboc*, ch. 16 (ed. Spindler, p. 184); *VI Æthelred*, ch. 7, ed. Liebermann, *Gesetze*, vol. I, p. 248.

that broad definition to examine a wide range of practices which early medieval people did *not* themselves regard as magical.[162] Other scholars, notably Richard Kieckhefer, have subsequently objected that 'it seems particularly unhelpful to use a historical term in a way that not only differs from but actually conflicts with its historical usage', and argued that our approach should instead pay more attention to how and why medieval people distinguished magic from other forms of ritual, practice, and entreaty.[163] Quite understandably, debates of this kind have encouraged others simply to avoid the term where possible, and to propose alternative labels for the material they wish to investigate, as Audrey Meaney's study of 'extra-medical elements' in Old English remedy-collections sought to do as a way to bring 'amulets, incantations and rituals' of all kinds within a single analytical category.[164]

It remains valuable nonetheless to acknowledge that a wide variety of early medieval writers were perfectly willing to characterize some kinds of activities as 'magical', and to ask what they meant by that characterization when they deployed it. Of fundamental importance to them, as Richard Kieckhefer has brought out with particular clarity, was their conviction that magical practices were those which operated according to 'either a sinister or an occult rationality'.[165] That certainly chimes well with the distinction which we have heard Augustine and Ælfric making about the proper and improper uses of plants to restore human health. They had not objected to all uses of plants in healing, but only to those in which it was hard to see how the cure had been achieved by the plant's own potency, and which relied instead on some process which was certainly occult (a word which we should take, as Kieckhefer advises us, to mean simply 'hidden, or non-manifest') and quite possibly also sinister (since one could not therefore rule out the possibility that demons might have been involved in bringing it about). A prerequisite of engaging in these ways of thinking was, therefore, the careful consideration of 'natural' causes and effects, to determine whether they were sufficient to explain how certain outcomes had been produced, or whether there must instead have been 'hidden or non-manifest' forces also at work.

These ways of thinking about magic and nature informed another of Ælfric's homilies, in which he expressed his concerns about the impious things 'which witches teach' about the leaving of offerings beside stones and trees.[166] His concerns had been stoked by his study of earlier Christian writings, which had firmly denounced such practices.[167] Ælfric seems to have thought that their

---

[162] Flint, *Rise of Magic*, p. 1.   [163] Kieckhefer, 'Specific rationality', p. 824.
[164] Meaney, 'Extra-medical elements'.   [165] Kieckhefer, 'Specific rationality', p. 816.
[166] Ælfric, *Lives of the Saints*, XVI.2 (ed. Clayton and Mullins, vol. II, p. 128).
[167] See Meaney, 'Sources', pp. 486–7.

message remained relevant to late tenth-century churchgoers, and his homily reiterated the view that no Christian should participate in such things. He justified his conclusion not, however, by appealing to the long line of earlier thinkers who had taken the same position, but rather by asking his audience to consider the natural capabilities of the stones and trees upon which the rites focused. Anyone who thought it profitable to participate in such activities ought, scoffed Ælfric, to have thought more seriously about 'how this dead stone or that dumb tree would be able to help them'.[168] The inability of stones and trees to perceive or respond to offerings was, in Ælfric's eyes, enough to discredit the practice entirely. He chose not to say outright whether that was because it was bound therefore to be ineffectual (and hence superstitious), or whether instead it could only be said to work through the operation of some 'hidden or non-manifest' force (and hence magical). Either way, it was again through a consideration of the natural capabilities of things that Ælfric thought he could pass judgement on the validity of other people's ritual actions.

How many of Ælfric's contemporaries really were in the habit of leaving offerings beside trees and stones, we cannot know; but sometimes within contemporary English manuscripts we do encounter instructions about the value of *speaking* to plants and other seemingly non-sentient things while one put them to use. To avoid fatigue while travelling, for instance, *Bald's Leechbook* recommended using mugwort, to which one should first 'say these words before the sun rises: "I will take you, mugwort, so that I do not become tired on the road"'.[169] Other collections gave similar instructions about the need to declare one's intentions to particular kinds of plants at the moment that one uprooted them, 'so that you come to me gladly with your powers blooming'.[170] It was generally taken, however, that plants lacked the capacity to perceive sound. A number of early medieval biblical commentators pointed out that if they could, then the Book of Genesis would surely have said that God had spoken to them in the way that he spoke to animals and to humans: but 'because trees do not have the sense of thinking or understanding ... then he did not therefore say to them "Increase and multiply"'.[171] What it meant to speak to plants in the manner sometimes recommended in early medieval herbaria is likely, therefore, to have raised questions for anyone who was otherwise confident that perception and sentience belonged exclusively to other kinds of

---

[168] Ælfric, *Lives of the Saints*, XVI.2 (ed. Clayton and Mullins, vol. II, p. 128).
[169] *Bald's Leechbook*, I.86.1 (ed. Cockayne, vol. II, p. 154).
[170] *Old English Herbarium*, ch. 179.1 (ed. D'Aronco, p. 354). Cf. also *Old English Herbarium*, chs. 19.4 and 176.1 (pp. 100 and 348); and *Lacnunga*, ch. 76 (ed. Niles, pp. 468–74). See also Garner, *Hybrid Healing*, pp. 129–59.
[171] *De sex dierum creatione* (ed. Migne, col. 217); Wigbod, *Liber quaestionum super librum Genesis* (ed. Migne, col. 1135).

beings. Here, one suspects, was another opportunity for worries like those voiced by Augustine and Ælfric to arise, about the causal principles by which these speech acts could be said to have achieved their effects.

Preachers who took up these sorts of issues in their sermons were frequently motivated by a sense that error often resulted from inattention. Congregations required instruction about what did and did not constitute magic, they thought, because they might give insufficient thought to *how* certain practices worked before they deployed them. Early medieval churchmen nevertheless also recognized that it was possible to overreact to the dangers of magic as well, by wrongly supposing that sinister forces lurked behind perfectly mundane customs and acts. If, for instance, it was necessary to divide land or other property between a number of people, one possible way of doing so might be to determine each person's share through the casting of lots. Yet early medieval Christians were frequently reminded that lot-casting numbered among the practices favoured by pagans and non-Christians, who might use it also as a means of determining the will of the gods or the shape of the future. The association between lot-casting and unchristian practices seems for some to have rendered the whole practice inescapably problematic, to the extent that some early medieval English Christians felt unwilling to wholeheartedly endorse even the stories found in the biblical book of Acts, and elsewhere, about the willingness of Christ's apostles to engage in the practice.[172] Did all this mean, therefore, that it would be best for the faithful to avoid the whole business altogether, no matter the purpose which the casting of lots was meant to serve? Ælfric of Eynsham anticipated that some of his contemporaries might need reassurance on exactly this question. In the same sermon as he had warned his congregation to disregard anything 'which witches teach', he spoke encouragingly about the possibility of 'casting lots with faith, without witchcraft, when it is in worldly things, so that if people are wanting to divide something up, the lot will determine for them'. Such a practice had, for Ælfric, only a superficial similarity with those of 'the heathens who cast lots about themselves with the Devil's art, which will destroy them forever'. His words drew attention not only to the intentions of participants but also to the underlying mechanics. He was content to think that lots only *sometimes* fell as they did according to 'the Devil's art', and presumably he therefore took pure chance to be responsible in other cases. If one set aside their divinatory applications, one could find them both safe and profitable: a lot which fell by chance was 'no sorcery, but is very often a means of direction'.[173]

---

[172] See Wright, 'Jewish magic', pp. 191–3.

[173] Ælfric, *Lives of the Saints*, XVI.2 (ed. Clayton and Mullins, vol. II, p. 124). For the originality of Ælfric's distinctions in this part of the sermon, and his independence from his major sources, see Meaney, 'Sources', pp. 481 and 493.

What Ælfric was offering to his listeners in these various discussions of magical practices, then, were a series of invitations to look deeper into the workings of things. Magical and non-magical acts might sometimes superficially resemble one another, but could be distinguished if one thought carefully about how, and by what means, they achieved their effects. Ælfric was not the only early medieval English writer to hold that view, and nor were sermons the only place in which one might find it being expressed. It was equally recognizable to the writers of saints' Lives, who were not unaware that the wondrous deeds of the saints might outwardly resemble some form of magic. One English hagiographer, translating the Life of St Guthlac from Latin into the vernacular, thought it likely that news of the miracles which Guthlac was performing in the fens would have prompted the saint's contemporaries to debate among themselves 'whether Guthlac did these things in the power of God, or through the craft of the Devil'.[174] There were good grounds for caution when it came to claims about miracle-workers. Some of the old stories about the deeds of the apostles reported, for instance, that the ancient sorcerer Simon had once sowed dissent against St Peter, precisely by undeservedly commanding the opinion of many people 'who marvelled at Simon's wondrous deeds' (his *wundordæde*, as one Old English version of the story put it), and who had failed to recognize that those wonders had in fact been achieved illicitly through magic.[175] In the case of St Guthlac and his own wonder-working, it was said that a man named Wigfrith took it upon himself to investigate the true nature of Guthlac's deeds. He considered himself to possess a certain expertise in the matter, having spent time in Ireland amongst a great many authentic miracle-workers as well as, according to the original Latin version of the story, a number of 'false hermits and pretenders of various religions'. Like the ancient Simon, those pretenders had indeed been able to perform apparent wonders of their own, but Wigfrith said that 'he did not know by what power' they did so.[176] That seems to have been enough for Wigfrith to draw his conclusions about their falsity, and readers of the Life were presumably expected to agree that any power which remained impervious to scrutiny ought to be distrusted.

Although hagiographers did therefore recognize the possibility that the inattentive might confuse miracle for magic, they seem to have been more deeply concerned by the possibility that some of their miracle-stories might

---

[174] *Prose Life of St Guthlac* (ed. Kramer, Magennis, and Norris, pp. 194–6); cf. Felix, *Vita Guthlaci*, ch. 46 (ed. Colgrave, p. 142).

[175] *Blickling Homilies*, ed. Morris, p. 173 [homily XV], following the version of the story told in the *Passio sanctorum apostolorum Petri et Pauli*, ch. 11 (ed. Lipsius, pp. 129–31). For other indications of engagement with the *Passio* in early medieval England, see the entry in Biggs (ed.), *Apocrypha*, p. 52.

[176] Felix, *Vita Guthlaci*, ch. 46 (ed. Colgrave, pp. 142–4).

simply be explained away as pure coincidence, and thus perfectly explicable as happenstance rather than as compelling evidence of divine intervention. The late eleventh-century archdeacon Herman was unusually direct in stating that possibility outright, when he insisted that certain events in the life of St Edmund ought to be understood as miraculous, even though 'it is commonly said that these things would have happened anyway'.[177] The corpus of earlier English saints' Lives certainly contains many episodes which were perfectly capable of generating this sort of reaction. The fortuitous recovery of a sheet of parchment, dropped by a crow over the marshes surrounding St Guthlac's fenland retreat, was celebrated as a miracle in the saint's Life on the basis that the sheet had landed safely among the reeds, and so had been retrieved before it suffered any water damage.[178] In much the same way, the Life of St Æthelwold later told how a lighted candle had fallen onto the saint's book, and 'revealed the holy man's merit' when the pages were left unharmed by it.[179] When the saints were petitioned by others, long after their deaths, hagiographers and miracle-collectors were just as inclined to celebrate the quiet fulfilment of prayers as they were to report the more spectacular manifestations of divine presence. A man bound in chains who came to pray for the assistance of St Swithun at Winchester found that as he knelt down beside the saint's tomb, the bolt fell from his shackles.[180] To any reader who might be tempted to offer a mundane explanation for how events of this kind could have happened, St Swithun's hagiographer Lantfred had a blunt message: 'envious and doubtful people, who deny the glorious miracles of this holy man ..., should be silent!'[181]

It can be easy to suppose that assertion was a hagiographer's primary mode of argumentation. Writing in his *Child's History of England* during the 1850s about the claims which had once been advanced about the saintliness of Archbishop Dunstan, the English novelist Charles Dickens took the view that the early medieval monks of Canterbury had simply 'settled that he was a Saint, and called him Saint Dunstan ever afterwards. They might just as well have settled that he was a coach-horse, and could just as easily have called him one'.[182] As it happens, the first Life of St Dunstan in fact stands as a particularly good example of the clear-sightedness with which hagiographers could anticipate, and therefore hope to forestall, potentially sceptical assessments of the miracles which they sought to attribute to the saints. Its author – the cleric who

---

[177] Herman, *Miracula Eadmundi*, ch. 13 (ed. Licence, pp. 30–2).
[178] Felix, *Vita Guthlaci*, ch. 37 (ed. Colgrave, pp. 116–18).
[179] Wulfstan of Winchester, *Vita Æthelwoldi*, ch. 36 (ed. Lapidge and Winterbottom, p. 54).
[180] Lantfred, *Translatio*, ch. 39 (ed. Lapidge, p. 332).
[181] Lantfred, *Translatio*, ch. 4 (ed. Lapidge, p. 286).
[182] Dickens, *Child's History of England*, vol. I, pp. 50–1. I owe this reference to Parish, 'Impudent and abhominable fictions', p. 45.

signed himself only as 'B.' whom we have already encountered in Section 2 – was evidently aware that several of his miracle-stories were vulnerable to being explained away in some manner. He knew, for instance, that some of the stranger things which Dunstan had said during his lifetime could be understood as 'empty ravings' and not, as B. now hoped to show, as prophetic revelations.[183] He also knew that other events from Dunstan's life might just as readily be attributed to some mundane or naturalistic explanation as to an otherworldly one. A stone had once narrowly missed Dunstan's head, B. said, after being thrown through the air from some unknown source. B. was well aware that one possible explanation for the act was simply that some human hand must have thrown it, whether carelessly or in malice. B.'s own view, however, was that the stone had been thrown by the Devil. In support of this claim, B. remarked upon a number of physical details which he felt bore out the interpretation. The stone was extremely heavy, for a start, and it could only be lifted with difficulty. More telling was the fact that 'there was no stone of its kind, large or small, in these parts of Somerset, as many people can attest', and it was this, said B., which 'clearly showed whose was the wicked hand which had sent it on its way'.[184] Hagiographers like B. attended closely to the persuasiveness of their claims, and thought that the workings of the supernatural could be most clearly discerned if one was able to render implausible any naturalistic alternatives.

It was often said that the saints, during their lifetimes, had had to exercise exactly this sort of discernment in their own encounters with the supernatural. Their perceptiveness in recognizing things for what they were, rather than what they seemed to be, was regularly celebrated by their hagiographers. Another of the stories told by B. about St Dunstan, for instance, was that the Devil had once tried to interrupt the saint's prayers by appearing in the forms of various animals, first as a bear, then as a dog, a dragon, and a fox. None of these disguises made the slightest difference, however, and Dunstan saw through each in turn, recognizing the true nature of his opponent 'with spiritual rather than bodily sight'.[185] Similar claims about saintly perception could already be found in the very earliest English saints' Lives, inspired by influential scenes from late antique hagiography. Even when the saints did rely upon their bodily senses, they were often said to have exercised a clarity of judgement which took in tell-tale signs that ordinary men and women might have missed. St Cuthbert's early eighth-century hagiographers claimed that the saint had once ministered to a stranger in his monastery's guesthouse on one winter's morning, but soon

---

[183] B., *Vita Dunstani*, ch. 33 (ed. Winterbottom and Lapidge, p. 96).
[184] B., *Vita Dunstani*, ch. 18 (ed. Winterbottom and Lapidge, pp. 58–60).
[185] B., *Vita Dunstani*, ch. 16 (ed. Winterbottom and Lapidge, pp. 54–6).

Figure 10 Illusory fire disrupts St Cuthbert's preaching, in an illustrated copy of Bede's *Vita Cuthberti* (Oxford, University College, MS 165, p. 43). By permission of the Master and Fellows of University College, Oxford.

noticed that his guest had left no footprints in the snow, and so 'understood that he had been an angel of God'.[186] The version of the story told by Bede described the saint inspecting loaves of bread left by his guest, judging from their physical characteristics that they were 'of a kind that the earth is unable to produce', and leading him therefore to the conclusion that 'it is evident from this that they have not come from our own soil, but been brought the paradise of joy'.[187] Ordinary people, by contrast, might too easily overlook these sorts of indications, and so arrive at mistaken conclusions about what they saw or experienced. Phantom flames had once engulfed a house in a Northumbrian village at which St Cuthbert was preaching, in an illusion wrought by Devil to disrupt the saint's teaching (Figure 10). The villagers who ran to extinguish the blaze only realised the truth when they noticed that the flames were not burning in the usual manner: there was 'no trace of the smoke which appears before and after fire, and they realised that they had been deceived'.[188] Natural and supernatural phenomena might sometimes seem to closely resemble each other, but

---

[186] *Vita Cuthberti*, II.2 (ed. Colgrave, pp. 76–8).
[187] Bede, *Vita Cuthberti*, ch. 7 (ed. Colgrave, pp. 176–8).
[188] *Vita Cuthberti*, II.6 (ed. Colgrave, pp. 86–8).

hagiographers expressed confidence that with careful attention, it was possible to correctly distinguish the one from the other.

In the Lives of the saints, just as much as in sermons warning about the dangers of magic, early medieval English men and women were thus frequently encouraged to give extended thought to natural processes and behaviours, in order to set them against other kinds of occurrences which needed to be understood differently. We should not imagine that this kind of thinking took place only in and around texts. Our sources occasionally indicate how it could also carry over into spoken conversations and interpersonal debate as well. The Welsh bishop Asser (d. 908/9) recalled the swirl of speculation that had gathered around discussions of a mysterious illness from which Alfred, king of Wessex, suffered for much of his adult life.[189] He included both the illness and the rumours in his biography of Alfred, composed – unusually – while the king still lived and reigned. It had been during Alfred's wedding-feast that the king had suddenly been gripped by unexpected and severe pains. Some of those who were there, and others who swiftly heard about it for themselves, thought that Alfred had been struck by 'some unfamiliar kind of fever', or believed that there must have been a connection with the ailments which Alfred had previously suffered in childhood. Others however 'claimed that it had happened through the influence and enchantment (*fauore et fascinatione*) of the people gathered around', or otherwise attributed it to 'the ill will of the Devil, who can always become envious of good people'.[190] Although there was conjecture, there was no consensus. As a close associate of Alfred's, Asser had his own opinions about what had happened and in his Life of the king, he alerted his readers to important details about Alfred's devotional habits, which he believed cast the whole situation in a new light.[191]

Real-life events and contemporary circumstances were here prompting the inhabitants of Alfred's kingdom to think about the subtle and contestable differences between natural and supernatural explanations of the same phenomena, no less effectively than the words of any homilist or hagiographer. They speculated and hypothesized, arriving at individual judgements – some naturalistic, others not – which seemed to them to make the best sense of the circumstances as they understood them. Public opinion had swiftly splintered over the issue, yet there was still the possibility, according to some, that the true explanation might one day be found among all the competing theories. Fresh efforts were still being made 'even today', said Asser, to try to 'determine ... where this ailment

---

[189] Asser, *Vita Alfredi*, ch. 74 (ed. Stevenson, pp. 54–5).
[190] On Asser's reference to magical intervention, I follow the interpretation proposed by Meaney, 'Anglo-Saxon view', pp. 22–3.
[191] See Pratt, 'Illnesses'.

had come from' once and for all. In their conviction that the matter would one day be resolved beyond doubt, the inhabitants of this early medieval kingdom displayed not only their curiosity about the many different kinds of forces which were capable of affecting their world, but also their confidence that human intellects would surely, in the end, be equal to the task of telling them apart.

Final Thoughts

Early medieval thinkers sometimes reflected on the degree to which their understanding of the world had been shared by previous generations. Probably, some suggested, it had been easier in the past to imagine that the world was stranger and more inexplicable than it really was. Rational good sense now made educated men and women wary of accepting many of the things with which the more credulous ancients had been prepared to believe as fact. This was the opinion of one late seventh- or early eighth-century English writer who had scoured the works of ancient authors looking for stories about monsters and marvels, and who had come away from his task with a deep sense of scepticism about what he had been reading. He collected together what he had found into his own *Liber monstrorum* ('The Book of Monsters'), but immediately cautioned his readers that 'only some things among these marvels are believed to be true' and that very many more were wholly fanciful. 'If someone was able to take flight on wings and search them out', he said, they would soon find that 'there in the place where there are said to be a golden city and shores scattered with jewels, one would discover only shores made of rocks and a city of stone – or no city at all'.[192] The author of the *Liber monstrorum* thought that 'the deceitful tales of poets who willingly invent many things which do not occur' were chiefly to blame for these spurious fictions about faraway marvels.[193] Others observed instead the ease with which misunderstandings might generate supernatural explanations for perfectly mundane natural phenomena, and felt confident that they themselves possessed a fuller and more accurate understanding of the world that guarded them against such credulity. Where once sailors in the Mediterranean had convinced themselves that they could hear the terrifying sounds of the monstrous Scylla over the crashing waves, a well-read early medieval scholar like Bede could feel certain without even leaving their library that the true explanation was likely to be found instead in the movements of air stimulated by the fires of Mount Etna.[194]

---

[192] *Liber monstrorum*, preface (ed. Orchard, pp. 254–6). On this aspect of the work, see Orchard, *Pride and Prodigies*, pp. 87–94; and Weaver, 'Canterbury school', pp. 75–83.

[193] *Liber monstrorum*, III.23 (ed. Orchard, p. 314).

[194] Bede, *De natura rerum*, ch. 50 (ed. Jones, p. 233); drawing on Isidore, *De natura rerum*, ch. 47 (ed. Fontaine, pp. 321–3).

In much the same way, the catalogues of herbs and their properties which early medieval men and women had at their disposal offered a grounding in the natural characteristics of plants which could save them from embarrassing errors – by informing them, for instance, that some kinds of plant shone with starlike brightness at night-time, and that people who were ignorant of that fact often mistook their glowing light for some kind of phantasmal apparition (to the amusement of local shepherds who knew better).[195] To encounter remarks of these kinds in one's books was to be given every reason to consider oneself better informed and less prone to fantastical conjecture than the individuals who had had to make sense of the world without the assistance of such helpful and clear-sighted authorities.

Early medieval men and women knew, in other words, that the stories which people told about the world could change. By ranging widely across the period between the seventh century and the eleventh in this Element, looking for the kinds of situations which prompted early medieval English thinkers to make distinctions between what was 'natural' and what was not, we inevitably obscure the degree to which the convictions expressed in our sources were themselves subject to change during this long period. Although I have suggested that a substantial number of people across the early Middle Ages found themselves asking comparable questions about things that lay, as Bede once wrote, 'beyond the natural', they need not have agreed in every particular about where precisely the boundaries of the 'natural' ought to be set. A reader of saints' Lives in the early eighth century might reasonably have concluded that those boundaries were currently undergoing expansion, and that efforts were presently underway to return the world to an increasingly 'natural' state. Contemporary hagiographers were telling stories, after all, about the various saints who had recently succeeded in expelling demons from pockets of wilderness all over Britain, curtailing the activities of otherworldly beings and removing all trace of their malign influence upon the landscape.[196] But by the end of the period, in contrast, it might have seemed that the supernatural was being brought *closer* to hand instead, through the expanding repertoire of benedictional formulae by which English churchmen could ask for God's blessing upon trees and fruit, houses and fields – some seeking, as Helen Gittos has put it, to 'permanently change the character of an area of open land' through new interventions of the divine within the physical world.[197]

---

[195] *Old English Herbarium*, ch. 61 (ed. D'Aronco, p. 166); cf. pseudo-Apuleius, *Herbarius*, ch. 60 (ed. Howald and Sigerist, p. 114).
[196] See Brooks, *Restoring Creation*.
[197] Gittos, *Liturgy*, p. 39. See also Rowe, 'Blessings for nature'.

A society's perceived relationship with the supernatural need not develop unidirectionally, and as individual clusters of beliefs and practices underwent their own incremental changes across this period, the conclusions which contemporaries drew when they considered them all in aggregate had the potential to shift in unexpected and unpredictable ways.

Of all the conclusions posited by the individuals examined here, it is the brief comment made by Alcuin about the nature of the physical world to which I have found myself most frequently returning while writing this Element. In a striking image, offered to the Frankish prince Pippin in the course of an educational *Disputatio* written towards the end of the eighth century, Alcuin said that the earth (*terra*) might be thought of as 'the mother of the growing, the nurse of the living, the storeroom of life, and the devourer of all things' (*mater crescentium, nutrix uiuentium, cellarium uitae, deuoratrix omnium*).[198] Alcuin's formulation, as so often, was not wholly his own: he had modelled his question-and-answer text on a much older Latin source, which had already suggested the central connection between the earth and the sustenance of living beings. Alcuin re-used what his source had suggested to him – 'What is the earth? A storeroom for life' (*Quid est terra? Cellarium uite*) – and sought to expand upon it.[199] His final image was a complex and disquieting one, which followed a changing relationship between the physical world and the creatures which it first nurtured into maturity, and then swallowed up with grim inevitability. Echoes of earlier Anglo-Latin poetry, which had already likened processes of earthly decay to monstrous cyclopes gulping down their meals, suggest where Alcuin had taken inspiration for some of his expanded imagery.[200] But for Alcuin to settle at last upon the suggestion that the earth was the devourer of *everything* is, I think, unexpected. He had grown up with people who had claimed to have seen angels with their own eyes; and he expressed his certainty to some of his monastic correspondents that the souls of the dead surely still watched over them, looking down upon their old homes while they lived on in the presence of God.[201] There *were* things beyond this ravenous earth, he was sure. The task of describing them had long been taken up by speakers of Old English, and traces of how they did so still linger in the words which they coined for the purpose when they found it necessary, as Alaric Hall has put it, 'to speak of what we might call "otherworlds"'.[202] It would be understandable, nonetheless, if sometimes it was

---

[198] See Section 1.
[199] *Altercatio Hadriani*, 47 (ed. Suchier, p. 106). See also Orchard, 'Alcuin's educational dispute'.
[200] Aldhelm, *Enigmata*, C (ed. Ehwald, p. 147).
[201] Visions of angels: Alcuin, *Versus de patribus*, lines 1597–1648 (ed. Godman, pp. 128–32); see Sowerby, *Angels*, pp. 168–70. Souls of the dead: Alcuin, *Epistolae*, CCLXXXIV (ed. Dümmler, pp. 442–3).
[202] See Hall, 'Etymology'.

the condition of *this* world which most fully occupied their minds, as perhaps it had done for Alcuin as he searched for ways to express the facts of life for a young Frankish prince. The ideas which early medieval men and women generated about those 'other worlds' and what they might contain were informed, inescapably, by what they found in their own.

Bibliography

Primary Sources

Ælfric, *Catholic Homilies* (first series), ed. Peter Clemoes, *Ælfric's Catholic Homilies: The First Series*, Early English Text Society, s.s. 17 (Oxford: Oxford University Press, 1997).

Ælfric, *De temporibus anni*, ed. and trans. Martin Blake, *Ælfric's De temporibus anni*, Anglo-Saxon Texts 6 (Cambridge: D. S. Brewer, 2009).

Ælfric, *Lives of the Saints*, ed. and trans. Mary Clayton and Juliet Mullins, *Ælfric: Old English Lives of the Saints*, Dumbarton Oaks Medieval Library 58–60, 3 vols. (Cambridge: Harvard University Press, 2019).

Æthelwulf, *De abbatibus*, ed. and trans. Alistair Campbell, *Æthelwulf: De abbatibus* (Oxford: Clarendon Press, 1967).

Alcuin, *Disputatio Pippini*, ed. Walther Suchier, in Lloyd William Daly and Walther Suchier, *Altercatio Hadriani Augusti et Epicteti philosophi* (Urbana: University of Illinois Press, 1939), pp. 134–46.

Alcuin, *Epistolae*, ed. Ernst Dümmler, *Epistolae Karolini aevi: Tomus II*, Monumenta Germaniae Historica, Epistolae 4 (Berlin: Weidmann, 1895), pp. 18–481.

Alcuin, *Versus de patribus regibus et sanctis Euboricensis ecclesiae*, ed. and trans. Peter Godman, *Alcuin: The Bishops, Kings and Saints of York* (Oxford: Clarendon Press, 1982).

Aldhelm, *Enigmata*, ed. Rudolf Ehwald, *Aldhelmi opera*, Monumenta Germaniae Historica, Auctores antiquissimi 15 (Berlin: Weidmann, 1919), pp. 99–149.

Aldhelm, *Epistola ad Acircium*, ed. Rudolf Ehwald, *Aldhelmi opera*, Monumenta Germaniae Historica, Auctores antiquissimi 15 (Berlin: Weidmann, 1919), pp. 33–204.

Aldhelm: The Poetic Works, trans. Michael Lapidge and James L. Rosier (Cambridge: D. S. Brewer, 1985).

Altercatio Hadriani Augusti et Epicteti philosophi, ed. Walther Suchier, in Lloyd William Daly and Walther Suchier, *Altercatio Hadriani Augusti et Epicteti philosophi* (Urbana: University of Illinois Press, 1939), pp. 101–10.

Ambrose, *Exameron*, ed. Karl Schenkl, *Sancti Ambrosii opera: Pars I*, Corpus scriptorum ecclesiasticorum latinorum 32.1 (Vienna: F. Tempsky, 1896), pp. 3–261.

Asser, *Vita Alfredi*, ed. William Henry Stevenson, *Asser's Life of King Alfred, Together with the Annals of Saint Neots Erroneously Ascribed to Asser* (Oxford: Clarendon Press, 1904).

Augustine, *De ciuitate Dei*, ed. Bernhard Dombart and Alfons Kalb, *Sancti Aurelii Augustini episcopi De civitate Dei*, Corpus christianorum series latina 47–8 (Turnhout: Brepols, 1955).

Augustine, *De diuersis quaestionibus octoginta tribus*, ed. Almut Mutzenbecher, *Sancti Aurelii Augustini opera: Pars XIII, 2*, Corpus christianorum series latina 44A (Turnhout: Brepols, 1975), pp. 1–249.

Augustine, *De doctrina christiana*, ed. and trans. Madeleine Moreau, Isabelle Bochet and Goulven Madec, *La doctrine chrétienne*, Œuvres de Saint Augustin 11.2 (Paris: Institut d'Études Augustiniennes, 1997).

Augustine, *De Genesi ad litteram*, ed. Joseph Zycha, *Sancti Aureli Augustini De Genesi ad litteram libri duodecim eiusdem libri capitula, De Genesi ad litteram inperfectus liber, Locutionum in Heptateuchum libri septem*, Corpus scriptorum ecclesiasticorum latinorum 28.1 (Vienna: F. Tempsky, 1894), pp. 1–456.

B., *Vita S. Dunstani*, ed. and trans. Michael Winterbottom and Michael Lapidge, *The Early Lives of St Dunstan* (Oxford: Clarendon Press, 2012), pp. 1–109.

Bald's Leechbook, ed. and trans. Oswald Cockayne, *Leechdoms, Wortcunning, and Starcraft of Early England*, Rolls Series 35, 3 vols. (London: Longman, 1864–1866), vol. 2, pp. 1–299.

Bazire, Joyce and James E. Cross (eds.), *Eleven Old English Rogationtide Homilies*, 2nd ed. (Exeter: Short Run Press, 1989).

Bede, *De natura rerum*, ed. Charles W. Jones, *Bedae Venerabilis opera: Pars I: opera didascalica*, Corpus christianorum series latina 123A (Turnhout: Brepols, 1975), pp. 173–234.

Bede, *De temporum ratione*, ed. Charles W. Jones, *Bedae Venerabilis opera: Pars VI: opera didascalia, 2*, Corpus christianorum series latina 123B (Turnhout: Brepols, 1977).

Bede, *Expositio actuum apostolorum*, ed. Max L. W. Laistner, *Bedae Venerabilis opera: Pars II: opera exegetica, 4*, Corpus christianorum series latina 121 (Turnhout: Brepols, 1983), pp. 1–99.

Bede, *Homilia*, ed. David Hurst, *Bedae Venerabilis opera. Pars III: opera homiletica. Pars IV: opera rhythmica*, Corpus christianorum series latina 122 (Turnhout: Brepols, 1955), pp. 1–378.

Bede, *In epistulas septem catholicas*, ed. David Hurst, *Bedae Venerabilis opera: Pars II: opera exegetica, 4*, Corpus christianorum series latina 121 (Turnhout: Brepols, 1983), pp. 179–342.

Bede, *In Genesim*, ed. Charles W. Jones, *Bedae Venerabilis opera. Pars II: opera exegetica, 1*, Corpus christianorum series latina 118A (Turnhout: Brepols, 1967).

Bede, *In Marci evangelium expositio*, ed. David Hurst, *Bedae Venerabilis opera: Pars II: opera exegetica, 3*, Corpus christianorum series latina 120 (Turnhout: Brepols, 1960), pp. 427–648.

Bede, *Vita S. Cuthberti*, ed. and trans. Bertram Colgrave, *Two Lives of Saint Cuthbert: A Life by an Anonymous Monk of Lindisfarne and Bede's Prose Life* (Cambridge: Cambridge University Press, 1940), pp. 141–307.

Beowulf, ed. Frederick Klaeber, *Beowulf and the Fight at Finnsburg*, 3rd ed. with supplements (Boston: D. C. Heath, 1950).

The Blickling Homilies, ed. and trans. Richard Morris, Early English Text Society, o.s. 58, 63 and 73 (London: Oxford University Press, 1874–1880); rptd in one volume (London: Oxford University Press, 1967).

Boethius, *De consolatione Philosophiae*, ed. Ludwig Bieler, *Anicii Manlii Severini Boethii Philosophiae Consolatio*, Corpus christianorum series latina 94 (Turnhout: Brepols, 1957).

Byrhtferth, *Enchiridion*, ed. and trans. Peter S. Baker and Michael Lapidge, *Byrhtferth's 'Enchiridion'*, Early English Text Society, s.s. 15 (Oxford: Oxford University Press, 1995).

Cassiodorus, *Expositio psalmorum*, ed. Marc Adriaen, *Magni Aurelii Cassiodori senatoris opera: Pars II*, Corpus christianorum series latina 97–8 (Turnhout: Brepols, 1958).

Cath Maige Tuired, ed. and trans. Elizabeth A. Gray, *Cath Maige Tuired: The Second Battle of Mag Tuired*, Irish Texts Society 52 (London: Irish Texts Society, 1982).

Chardonnens, László Sándor (ed. and trans.), *Anglo-Saxon Prognostics, 900– 1100: Study and Texts*, Brill's Texts and Sources in Intellectual History 3 (Leiden: Brill, 2007).

Concilium Lateranense (649), ed. Rudolf Riedinger, *Concilium Laternanense a. 649 celebratum*, Acta conciliorum oecumenicorum II.1 (Berlin: De Gruyter, 1984).

De sex dierum creatione, ed. Jacques-Paul Migne, *Patrologia Latina* 93 (Paris: Migne, 1862), cols. 207–34.

Die Briefe des heiligen Bonifatius und Lullus, ed. Michael Tangl, Monumenta Germaniae Historica, Epistolae selectae I (Berlin: Weidmann, 1916).

'1 Enoch', trans. Matthew Black, *The Book of Enoch or 1 Enoch: A New English Edition* (Leiden: Brill, 1985).

Eustathius, *Hexaemeron*, ed. Emmanuel Amand de Mendieta and Stig Y. Rudberg, *Eustathius: Ancienne version latine des neuf homélies sur l'Hexaéméron de Basile de Césarée* (Berlin: Akademie Verlag, 1958).

The Exeter Anthology of Old English Poetry: An Edition of Exeter Dean and Chapter MS 3501, ed. Bernard J. Muir, 2 vols., 2nd ed. (Exeter: University of Exeter Press, 2000).

Felix, *Vita S. Guthlaci*, ed. and trans. Bertram Colgrave, *Felix's Life of St Guthlac* (Cambridge: Cambridge University Press, 1956).

Gregory the Great, *Dialogi*, ed. and trans. Adalbert de Vogüé, *Grégoire le Grand: Dialogues*, Sources Chrétiennes 251, 260, 265 (Paris: Éditions du Cerf, 1978–1980).

The Guthlac Poems of the Exeter Book, ed. Jane Roberts (Oxford: Oxford University Press, 1979).

Gysseling, Maurits (ed.), *Corpus van Middelnederlandse teksten (tot en met het jaar 1300). Reeks II: Literaire handschriften, Deel 1: Fragmenten* (The Hague: Martinus Nijhoff, 1980).

Helisachar of Trier, *Legimus in ecclesiasticis historiis*, ed. James E. Cross, '"Legimus in ecclesiasticis historiis": A sermon for All Saints, and its use in Old English prose', *Traditio* 33 (1977), 101–35.

Herman, *Miracula S. Eadmundi*, ed. and trans. Tom Licence, *Herman the Archdeacon and Goscelin of Saint-Bertin: Miracles of St Edmund* (Oxford: Clarendon Press, 2014), pp. 1–125.

Isidore, *De natura rerum*, ed. and trans. Jacques Fontaine, *Isidore de Seville: Traité de la nature* (Bordeaux: Féret et fils, 1960).

Lacnunga, ed. and trans. John D. Niles, in John D. Niles and Maria A. D'Aronco, *Medical Writings from Early Medieval England. Volume I: The Old English Herbal, Lacnunga, and Other Texts*, Dumbarton Oaks Medieval Library 81 (Cambridge: Harvard University Press, 2023), pp. 419–531.

Lantfred, *Translatio et miracula S. Swithuni*, ed. and trans. Michael Lapidge, *The Cult of St Swithun*, Winchester Studies IV.2 (Oxford: Clarendon Press, 2003), pp. 252–333.

Leechbook III, ed. and trans. Oswald Cockayne, *Leechdoms, Wortcunning, and Starcraft of Early England*, Rolls Series 35, 3 vols. (London: Longman, 1864–1866), vol. II, pp. 300–360.

Liber beatae Gregorii papae, ed. and trans. Bertram Colgrave, *The Earliest Life of Gregory the Great by an Anonymous Monk of Whitby* (Lawrence: University of Kansas Press, 1968).

Liber monstrorum, ed. and trans. Andy Orchard, *Pride and Prodigies: Studies in the Monsters of the Beowulf-Manuscript* (Cambridge: D. S. Brewer, 1985), pp. 254–317.

Liebermann, Felix (ed.), *Die Gesetze der Angelsachsen*, 3 vols. (Halle: Max Niemeyer, 1903–1916).

Liuzza, Roy M. (ed. and trans.), *Anglo-Saxon Prognostics: An Edition and Translation of Texts from London, British Library, MS Cotton Tiberius A.iii*, Anglo-Saxon Texts 9 (Cambridge: D. S. Brewer, 2010).

Medicina de quadrupedibus, ed. and trans. Maria A. D'Aronco, in John D. Niles and Maria A. D'Aronco, *Medical Writings from Early Medieval England. Volume I: The Old English Herbal, Lacnunga, and Other Texts*, Dumbarton Oaks Medieval Library 81 (Cambridge: Harvard University Press, 2023), pp. 367–417.

Napier, Arthur (ed.), *Wulfstan: Sammlung der ihm zugeschriebenen Homilien nebst Untersuchungen über ihre Echtheit*, Sammlung englischer Denkmäler in kritischen Ausgaben 4 (Berlin: Weidmann, 1883).

Old English Boethius, ed. and trans. Malcolm Godden and Susan Irvine, *The Old English Boethius: An Edition of the Old English Versions of Boethius's 'De consolatione Philosophiae'*, 2 vols. (Oxford: Oxford University Press, 2009).

Old English Dialogues of Gregory the Great, ed. Hans Hecht, *Bischofs Wærferth von Worcester Übersetzung der Dialoge Gregors des Grossen*, 2 vols. (Leipzig: George H. Wigand, 1900–1907).

The Old English Dialogues of Solomon and Saturn, ed. and trans. Daniel Anlezark, Anglo-Saxon Texts 7 (Woodbridge: Boydell and Brewer, 2009).

The 'Old English Heptateuch' and Ælfric's 'Libellus de veteri testamento et novo', ed. Richard Marsden, Early English Text Society, o.s. 330 (Oxford: Oxford University Press, 2008).

Old English Herbarium, ed. and trans. Maria A. D'Aronco, in John D. Niles and Maria A. D'Aronco, *Medical Writings from Early Medieval England. Volume I: The Old English Herbal, Lacnunga, and Other Texts*, Dumbarton Oaks Medieval Library 81 (Cambridge: Harvard University Press, 2023), pp. 1–365.

Old English Penitential, ed. Josef Raith, *Die altenglische Version des Halitgar'schen Bussbuches (sog. Poenitentiale Pseudo-Ecgberti)*, Bibliothek der angelsächsischen Prosa 13 (Hamburg: H. Grand, 1933; repr. Darmstadt: Wissenschaftliche Buchgesellschaft, 1964).

Paenitentiale Halitgarii, ed. Hermann Joseph Schmitz, *Die Bussbücher und die Bussdisciplin der Kirche*, 2 vols. (Mainz: Franz Kirchheim and L. Schwann, 1883–1898), vol. II, pp. 252–300.

Passio sanctorum apostolorum Petri et Pauli, ed. Richard Adelbert Lipsius, in Richard Adelbert Lipsius and Maximilien Bonnet, *Acta apostolorum apocrypha*, 2 parts in 3 vols. (Leipzig: Hermann Mendelssohn, 1891–1903), vol. I, pp. 119–77.

Pliny, *Naturalis historia*, ed. and trans. Harris Rackham, William H. S. Jones and David E. Eichholz, *Pliny: Natural History*, 10 vols. (Cambridge, MA: Harvard University Press, 1938–1963).

The Prayer Book of Aedeluald the Bishop, Commonly Called the Book of Cerne, ed. Arthur B. Kuypers (Cambridge: Cambridge University Press, 1902).

Prose Life of St Guthlac, ed. and trans. Johanna Kramer, Hugh Magennis and Robin Norris, *Anonymous Old English Lives of Saints*, Dumbarton Oaks Medieval Library 63 (Cambridge: Harvard University Press, 2020), pp. 141–217.

Pseudo-Apuleius, *Herbarius*, ed. Ernst Howald and Henry E. Sigerist, *Antonii Musae de herba vettonica, Liber pseudoapulei herbarius, Anonymi de taxone liber, Sexti Placiti liber medicinae ex animalibus*, Corpus Medicorum Latinorum 4 (Leipzig: Teubner, 1927), pp. 12–225.

Pseudo-Dionysius, *De diuinis nominibus*, ed. Beate Regina Suchla, *Corpus Dionysiacum I*, Patristische Texte und Studien 33 (Berlin: De Gruyter, 1990), pp. 93–231.

Pseudo-Dionysius, *Epistulae*, ed. Günter Heil and Adolf Martin Ritter, *Corpus Dionysiacum II*, Patristische Texte und Studien 36 (Berlin: De Gruyter, 1991), pp. 151–210.

Rituale ecclesiae Dunelmensis: The Durham Collectar, ed. Uno Lindelöf, Surtees Society 140 (Durham: Andrews, 1927).

Scriftboc, ed. Robert Spindler, *Das altenglische Bussbuch (sog. Confessionale Pseudo-Ecgberti): Ein Beitrag zu den kirchlichen Gesetzen der Angelsachsen* (Leipzig: Bernhard Tauchnitz, 1934).

Sex aetates mundi, ed. and trans. Dáibhí Ó Cróinín, *The Irish Sex Aetates Mundi* (Dublin: Dublin Institute for Advanced Studies, 1983).

Sextus Placitus, *Liber medicinae ex animalibus*, ed. Ernst Howald and Henry E. Sigerist, *Antonii Musae de herba vettonica, Liber pseudoapulei herbarius, Anonymi de taxone liber, Sexti Placiti liber medicinae ex animalibus*, Corpus Medicorum Latinorum 4 (Leipzig: Teubner, 1927), pp. 233–86.

Stephen, *Vita S. Wilfridi*, ed. and trans. Bertram Colgrave, *The Life of Bishop Wilfrid by Eddius Stephanus* (Cambridge: Cambridge University Press, 1927).

Storms, Godfrid (ed. and trans.), *Anglo-Saxon Magic* (The Hague: Martinus Nijhoff, 1948).

Theodorus Priscianus, *Euporiston*, ed. Valentin Rose, *Theodori Prisciani Euporiston libri III* (Leipzig: Teubner, 1894).

Vegetius, *Epitoma rei militaris*, ed. Michael D. Reeve, *Vegetius: Epitoma rei militaris* (Oxford: Oxford University Press, 2004).

The Vercelli Homilies and Related Texts, ed. Donald G. Scragg, Early English Texts Society, o.s. 300 (Oxford: Oxford University Press, 1992).

Vita S. Cuthberti, ed. and trans. Bertram Colgrave, *Two Lives of Saint Cuthbert: A Life by an Anonymous Monk of Lindisfarne and Bede's Prose Life* (Cambridge: Cambridge University Press, 1940), pp. 59–139.

Vita et miracula S. Kenelmi, ed. and trans. Rosalind C. Love, *Three Eleventh-Century Anglo-Latin Saints' Lives: Vita S. Birini, Vita et miracula S. Kenelmi, and Vita S. Rumwoldi* (Oxford: Clarendon Press, 1996), pp. 49–89.

Wigbod, *Liber quaestionum super librum Genesis*, ed. Migne, *Patrologia Latina* 96 (Paris: Migne, 1862), cols. 1105–68.

The Wonder of Creation, ed. and trans. Eric G. Stanley, '*The Wonder of Creation*: A new edition and translation, with discussion of problems', *Anglia* 131 (2013), 475–508.

Wulfstan, *Polity*, ed. and trans. Karl Jost, *Die 'Institutes of Polity, Civil and Ecclesiastical': Ein Werk Erzbischof Wulfstans von York*, Schweizer anglistische Arbeiten 47 (Bern: Francke, 1959).

Wulfstan of Winchester, *Vita S. Æthelwoldi*, ed. and trans. Michael Lapidge and Michael Winterbottom, *Wulfstan of Winchester: The Life of St Æthelwold* (Oxford: Clarendon Press, 1991).

Secondary Scholarship

Ahern, Eoghan, *Bede and the Cosmos: Theology and Nature in the Eighth Century* (London: Routledge, 2020).

Ahern, Eoghan, 'Bede's miracles reconsidered', *Early Medieval Europe* 26 (2018), 282–303.

Arthur, Ciaran, 'The heavenly field: A reconsideration of Mother Earth in the *Æcerbot* rite', *Journal of English and Germanic Philology* 122 (2023), 49–85.

Banham, Debby, 'Dun, Oxa and Pliny the great physician: Attribution and authority in Old English medical texts', *Social History of Medicine* 24 (2011), 57–73.

Banham, Debby and Rosamond Faith, *Anglo-Saxon Farms and Farming* (Oxford: Oxford University Press, 2014).

Bartlett, Robert, *The Natural and the Supernatural in the Middle Ages* (Cambridge: Cambridge University Press, 2008).

Bately, Janet M., 'Did King Alfred actually translate anything? The integrity of the Alfredian canon revisited', *Medium Ævum* 78 (2009), 189–215.

Biggs, Frederick M. (ed.), *Sources of Anglo-Saxon Literary Culture: The Apocrypha* (Kalamazoo: Medieval Institute, 2007).

Brooks, Britton Elliott, *Restoring Creation: The Natural World in the Anglo-Saxon Saints' Lives of Cuthbert and Guthlac* (Woodbridge: D. S. Brewer, 2019).

Bynum, Caroline Walker, *Jesus as Mother: Studies in the Spirituality of the High Middle Ages* (Berkeley: University of California Press, 1982).

Cameron, Malcolm L., *Anglo-Saxon Medicine* (Cambridge: Cambridge University Press, 1993).

Carney, James, *Studies in Irish Literature and History* (Dublin: Dublin Institute for Advanced Studies, 1955).

Cavell, Megan, 'A community of exiles: Whale and human domains in Old English poetry', in Susan McHugh, Robert McKay, and John Miller (eds.), *The Palgrave Handbook of Animals and Literature* (Cham: Palgrave Macmillan, 2021), pp. 97–110.

Chardonnens, László Sándor, 'Ælfric and the authorship of the Old English *De diebus malis*', in Concetta Giliberto and Loredana Teresi (eds.), *Limits to Learning: The Transfer of Encyclopaedic Knowledge in the Early Middle Ages* (Leuven: Peeters, 2013), pp. 123–53.

Chenu, Marie-Dominique, *Nature, Man, and Society: Essays on New Theological Perspectives in the Latin West*, ed. and trans. Jerome Taylor and Lester K. Little (Chicago: University of Chicago Press, 1968).

Christie, Edward J., 'The idea of an elephant: Ælfric of Eynsham, epistemology, and the absent animals of Anglo-Saxon England', *Neophilologus* 98 (2014), 465–79.

Clarke, Michael, 'The lore of the monstrous races in the developing text of the Irish *Sex Aetates Mundi*', *Cambrian Medieval Celtic Studies* 63 (2012), 15–49.

Cross, James E., 'The elephant to Alfred, Ælfric, Aldhelm and others', *Studia Neophilologica* 37 (1965), 367–73.

Daston, Lorraine, *Rules: A Short History of What We Live By* (Princeton: Princeton University Press, 2022).

de Lubac, Henri, *Surnaturel: Études historiques*, rev. Michel Sales (Paris: Desclée de Brouwer, 1991).

Dickens, Charles, *A Child's History of England*, 3 vols. (London: Bradbury and Evans, 1852–1854).

Durkheim, Émile, *Les Formes élémentaires de la vie religieuse: le système totémique en Australie* (Paris: Félix Alcan, 1912); trans. Joseph Ward Swain, *The Elementary Forms of the Religious Life*, 2nd ed. (London: Allen and Unwin, 1976).

Epstein, Stephen A., *The Medieval Discovery of Nature* (Cambridge: Cambridge University Press, 2012).

Flint, Valerie I. J., *The Rise of Magic in Early Medieval Europe* (Princeton: Princeton University Press, 1991).

Foxhall Forbes, Helen, *Heaven and Earth in Anglo-Saxon England: Theology and Society in an Age of Faith* (Farnham: Ashgate, 2013).

Garner, Lori Ann, *Hybrid Healing: Old English Remedies and Medical Texts* (Manchester: Manchester University Press, 2022).

Garrison, Mary, 'An insular copy of Pliny's *Naturalis historia* (Leiden VLF 4 fols 4–33)', in Erik Kwakkel (ed.), *Writing in Context: Insular Manuscript Culture 500–1200* (Leiden: Leiden University Press, 2013), pp. 67–125.

Gatch, Milton McC., 'Eschatology in the anonymous Old English homilies', *Traditio* 21 (1965), 117–65.

Gittos, Helen, *Liturgy, Architecture, and Sacred Places in Anglo-Saxon England* (Oxford: Oxford University Press, 2013).

Godden, Malcolm, 'Did King Alfred write anything?', *Medium Ævum* 76 (2007), 1–23.

Gordon, Stephen, *Supernatural Encounters: Demons and the Restless Dead in Medieval England, c. 1050–1450* (Abingdon: Routledge, 2020).

Green, Richard Firth, *Elf Queens and Holy Friars: Fairy Beliefs and the Medieval Church* (Philadelphia: University of Pennsylvania Press, 2016).

Hall, Alaric, *Elves in Anglo-Saxon England: Matters of Belief, Health, Gender and Identity* (Woodbridge: Boydell Press, 2007).

Hall, Alaric, 'The etymology and meanings of *eldritch*', *Scottish Language* 26 (2007), 16–22.

Hall, Alaric, 'The evidence for *maran*, the Anglo-Saxon "nightmares"', *Neophilologus* 91 (2007), 299–317.

Hall, Thomas N., 'The psychedelic transmogrification of the soul in Vercelli Homily IV', in Gerhard Jaritz and Gerson Moreno-Riaño (eds.), *Time and Eternity: The Medieval Discourse* (Turnhout: Brepols, 2003), pp. 309–22.

Heiduk, Matthias, Klaus Herbers, and Hans-Christian Lehner (eds.), *Prognostication in the Medieval World: A Handbook*, 2 vols. (Berlin: De Gruyter, 2021).

Hill, Thomas D., 'The *æcerbot* charm and its Christian user', *Anglo-Saxon England* 6 (1977), 213–21.

Hill, Thomas D., 'The falling leaf and buried treasure: Two notes on the imagery of *Solomon and Saturn*, 314–322', *Neuphilologische Mitteilungen* 71 (1970), 571–76.

Hines, John, 'Practical runic literacy in the late Anglo-Saxon period: Inscriptions on lead sheet', in Ursula Lenker and Lucia Kornexl (eds.), *Anglo-Saxon Micro-Texts* (Berlin: De Gruyter, 2019), pp. 29–59.

Jolly, Karen Louise, 'Anglo-Saxon charms in the context of a Christian world view', *Journal of Medieval History* 11 (1985), 279–93.

Jolly, Karen Louise, 'Father God and Mother Earth: Nature-mysticism in the Anglo-Saxon world', in Joyce E. Salisbury (ed.), *The Medieval World of Nature: A Book of Essays* (New York: Garland, 1993), pp. 221–52.

Jolly, Karen Louise, *Popular Religion in Late Saxon England: Elf Charms in Context* (Chapel Hill: University of North Carolina Press, 1996).

Jones, Christopher A., 'Furies, monks, and folklore in the earliest *miracula* of Saint Swithun', *Journal of English and Germanic Philology* 113 (2014), 407–42.

Kesling, Emily, *Medical Texts in Anglo-Saxon Literary Culture* (Cambridge: D. S. Brewer, 2020).

Keynes, Simon, 'An abbot, an archbishop, and the viking raids of 1006–7 and 1009–12', *Anglo-Saxon England* 36 (2007), 151–220.

Kieckhefer, Richard, 'The specific rationality of medieval magic', *American Historical Review* 99 (1994), 813–36.

Kitson, Peter, 'Lapidary traditions in Anglo-Saxon England: Part I, the background; the Old English Lapidary', *Anglo-Saxon England* 7 (1978), 9–60.

Lehoux, Daryn, 'Laws of nature and natural laws', *Studies in History and Philosophy of Science* 37 (2006), 527–49.

Leja, Meg, 'The sacred art: Medicine in the Carolingian renaissance', *Viator* 47 (2016), 1–34.

Lionarons, Joyce Tally, *The Homiletic Writings of Archbishop Wulfstan: A Critical Study* (Woodbridge: D. S. Brewer, 2010).

Markus, Robert A., 'Signs, communication, and communities in Augustine's *De doctrina christiana*', in Duane W. H. Arnold and Pamela Bright (eds.), *De doctrina christiana: A Classic of Western Culture* (Notre Dame: University of Notre Dame Press, 1995), pp. 97–108.

Meaney, Audrey L., 'Ælfric's use of his sources in his homily on auguries', *English Studies* 6 (1985), 477–95.

Meaney, Audrey L., 'The Anglo-Saxon view of the causes of illness', in Sheila Campbell, Bert Hall, and David Klausner (eds.), *Health, Disease and Healing in Medieval Culture* (Houndmills: Macmillan, 1992), pp. 12–33.

Meaney, Audrey L., 'Extra-medical elements in Anglo-Saxon medicine', *Social History of Medicine* 24 (2011), 41–56.

Mearns, Adam, 'This, that and the other: Locating the supernatural enemy in Old English', *English Language and Linguistics* 19 (2015), 213–26.

Mellinkoff, Ruth, 'Cain's monstrous progeny in *Beowulf*: Part I, Noachic tradition', *Anglo-Saxon England* 8 (1979), 143–62.

Mellinkoff, Ruth, 'Cain's monstrous progeny in *Beowulf*: Part II, post-diluvian survival', *Anglo-Saxon England* 9 (1981), 183–97.

Millard, Hannah Katherine, 'The significance of the *wyrm* in early medieval England', unpublished Ph.D. thesis, University of Birmingham (2021).

Mostert, Marco, 'Communicating the faith: The circle of Boniface, Germanic vernaculars, and Frisian and Saxon converts', *Amsterdamer Beiträge zur älteren Germanistik* 70 (2013), 87–130.

Murray, Alexander, *Reason and Society in the Middle Ages* (Oxford: Clarendon Press, 1978).

Neidorf, Leonard, 'Cain, Cam, Jutes, giants, and the textual criticism of *Beowulf*', *Studies in Philology* 112 (2015), 599–632.

Neidorf, Leonard and Kexin Zhang, 'Grendel and the witches: Germanic mythology and *Beowulf* line 163', *ANQ: A Quarterly Journal of Short Articles, Notes and Reviews* 37 (2024), 321–25.

Neville, Jennifer, *Representations of the Natural World in Old English Poetry* (Cambridge: Cambridge University Press, 1999).

Niles, John D., 'The *Ǽcerbot* ritual in context', in John D. Niles (ed.), *Old English Literature in Context* (Cambridge: D. S. Brewer, 1980), pp. 44–56.

O'Brien O'Keeffe, Katherine, '*Beowulf*, lines 702b–836: Transformations and the limits of the human', *Texas Studies in Language and Literature* 23 (1981), 484–94.

Orchard, Andy, 'Alcuin's educational dispute: The riddle of teaching and the teaching of riddles', in Susan Irvine and Winfried Rudolf (eds.), *Childhood and Adolescence in Anglo-Saxon Literary Culture* (Toronto: University of Toronto Press, 2018), pp. 162–201.

Orchard, Andy, *Pride and Prodigies: Studies in the Monsters of the Beowulf-Manuscript* (Cambridge: D. S. Brewer, 1985).

Parish, Helen L., '"Impudent and abhominable fictions": Rewriting saints' lives in the English Reformation', *Sixteenth Century Journal* 32 (2001), 45–65.

Peltola, Niilo, 'Grendel's descent from Cain reconsidered', *Neuphilologische Mitteilungen* 73 (1972), 284–91.

Pratt, David, 'The illnesses of King Alfred the Great', *Anglo-Saxon England* 30 (2001), 39–90.

Price, Richard, *The Acts of the Lateran Synod of 649* (Liverpool: Liverpool University Press, 2014).

Rauer, Christine, 'Female hagiography in the *Old English Martyrology*', in Paul Szarmach (ed.), *Writing Women Saints in Anglo-Saxon England* (Toronto: University of Toronto Press, 2013), pp. 13–29.

Ray, Roger, 'Who did Bede think he was?', in Scott DeGregorio (ed.), *Innovation and Tradition in the Writings of the Venerable Bede* (Morgantown: West Virginia University Press, 2006), pp. 11–36.

Rowe, Tamsin, 'Blessings for nature in the English liturgy, *c*. 900–1200', unpublished Ph.D. thesis, University of Exeter (2010).

Shaw, Richard, '"Just as the books tell us": A new work by Ælfric?', *Notes and Queries* 61 (2014), 328–36.

Sorrell, Paul, 'Like a duck to water: Representations of aquatic animals in early Anglo-Saxon literature and art', *Leeds Studies in English*, n.s. 25 (1994), 29–68.

Sowerby, Richard, *Angels in Early Medieval England* (Oxford: Oxford University Press, 2016).

Sowerby, Richard, 'When medicine doesn't work: Making sense of failure in the early Middle Ages', in Petros Bouras-Vallianatos and Zubin Mistry (eds.), *Ecologies of Healing in the Premodern World* (Edinburgh: Edinburgh University Press, forthcoming).

Thornbury, Emily V., 'Ælfric's zoology', *Neophilologus* 92 (2008), 141–53.

Wallis, Faith, '*Si naturam quæras*: Reframing Bede's "science"', in Scott DeGregorio (ed.), *Innovation and Tradition in the Writings of the Venerable Bede* (Morgantown: West Virginia University Press, 2006), pp. 65–99.

Watkins, Carl S., *History and the Supernatural in Medieval England* (Cambridge: Cambridge University Press, 2007).

Weaver, Erica, 'A Canterbury school of literary theory: Aldhelm's *De virginitate*, the *Liber monstrorum*, and (un)reliable fictions', in Daniel Donoghue, James Simpson, Nicholas Watson, and Anna Wilson (eds.), *The Practice and Politics of Reading, 650–1500* (Cambridge: D. S. Brewer, 2022), pp. 63–83.

Williams, Mark, *Ireland's Immortals: A History of Gods of Irish Myth* (Princeton: Princeton University Press, 2016).

Wright, Charles D., 'Jewish magic and Christian miracle in the Old English *Andreas*', in Samantha Zacher (ed.), *Imagining the Jew in Anglo-Saxon Literature and Culture* (Toronto: University of Toronto Press, 2016), pp. 167–93.

Acknowledgements

I would like to thank the series editors, together with Liz Friend-Smith at Cambridge University Press, first for inviting me to write this Element, and then most especially for their patience and understanding during the difficult circumstances over which it was written. I have profited from the advice and encouragement of the two anonymous reviewers in the final stages; and I owe particular thanks also to Zubin Mistry, who saved both me and the book during a moment of crisis, and who has been a constant source of support and good sense over many years. I have held onto the memory of old conversations with my dad, Steve Sowerby, which could always be depended upon to put things into their proper perspective, and I have missed him terribly while bringing this to a close. The basic shape of the book first suggested itself while I was pushing my younger daughter Erin over the fields in her pram; and she, her sister Holly, and my wife Stacey have waited too long for me to finish it off. It's time to go to the park.

England in the Early Medieval World

Megan Cavell
University of Birmingham

Megan Cavell is Associate Professor in Medieval English Literature at the University of Birmingham. She works on a wide range of topics in medieval literary studies, from Old and early Middle English and Latin languages and literature to riddling, gender and animal studies. Her previous publications include *Weaving Words and Binding Bodies: The Poetics of Human Experience in Old English Literature* (2016), *Riddles at Work in the Early Medieval Tradition: Words, Ideas, Interactions* (co-edited with Jennifer Neville, 2020), and *The Medieval Bestiary in England: Texts and Translations of the Old and Middle English Physiologus* (2022).

Rory Naismith
University of Cambridge

Rory Naismith is Professor of Early Medieval English History in the Department of Anglo-Saxon, Norse and Celtic at the University of Cambridge, and a Fellow of Corpus Christi College, Cambridge. Also a Fellow of the Royal Historical Society, he is the author of *Early Medieval Britain 500–1000* (Cambridge University Press, 2021), *Citadel of the Saxons: The Rise of Early London* (2018), *Medieval European Coinage, with a Catalogue of the Coins in the Fitzwilliam Museum, Cambridge, 8: Britain and Ireland c. 400–1066* (Cambridge University Press, 2017) and *Money and Power in Anglo-Saxon England: The Southern English Kingdoms 757–865* (Cambridge University Press, 2012, which won the 2013 International Society of Anglo-Saxonists First Book Prize).

Winfried Rudolf
University of Göttingen

Winfried Rudolf is Chair of Medieval English Language and Literature in the University of Göttingen (Germany). Recent publications include *Childhood and Adolescence in Anglo-Saxon Literary Culture* (with Susan E. Irvine, 2018). He has published widely on homiletic literature in early England and is currently principal investigator of the ERC-Project ECHOE–Electronic Corpus of Anonymous Homilies in Old English.

Emily V. Thornbury
Yale University

Emily V. Thornbury is Associate Professor of English at Yale University. She studies the literature and art of early England, with a particular emphasis on English and Latin poetry. Her publications include *Becoming a Poet in Anglo-Saxon England* (Cambridge, 2014), and, co-edited with Rebecca Stephenson, *Latinity and Identity in Anglo-Saxon Literature* (2016). She is currently working on a monograph called *The Virtue of Ornament*, about pre-Conquest theories of aesthetic value.

About the Series

Elements in England in the Early Medieval World takes an innovative, interdisciplinary view of the culture, history, literature, archaeology and legacy of England between the fifth and eleventh centuries. Individual contributions question and situate key themes, and thereby bring new perspectives to the heritage of early medieval England. They draw on texts in Latin and Old English as well as material culture to paint a vivid picture of the period. Relevant not only to students and scholars working in medieval studies, these volumes explore the rich intellectual, methodological and comparative value that the dynamic researchers interested in England between the fifth and eleventh centuries have to offer in a modern, global context. The series is driven by a commitment to inclusive and critical scholarship, and to the view that early medieval studies have a part to play in many fields of academic research, as well as constituting a vibrant and self-contained area of research in its own right.

Cambridge Elements

England in the Early Medieval World

Elements in the Series

Crime and Punishment in Anglo-Saxon England
Andrew Rabin

Europe and the Anglo-Saxons
Francesca Tinti

Art and the Formation of Early Medieval England
Catherine E. Karkov

Writing the World in Early Medieval England
Nicole Guenther Discenza and Heide Estes

Multilingualism in Early Medieval Britain
Lindy Brady

Recovering Old English
Kees Dekker

Health and the Body in Early Medieval England
Caroline Batten

Entertainment, Pleasure, and Meaning in Early England
Martha Bayless

Visions of Hierarchy and Inequality in Early Medieval England
Stuart Pracy

Literary Form in Early Medieval England
Jennifer A. Lorden

Natural and Supernatural in Early Medieval England
Richard Sowerby

A full series listing is available at: www.cambridge.org/EASW

For EU product safety concerns, contact us at Calle de José Abascal, 56–1°,
28003 Madrid, Spain or eugpsr@cambridge.org.

www.ingramcontent.com/pod-product-compliance
Ingram Content Group UK Ltd.
Pitfield, Milton Keynes, MK11 3LW, UK
UKHW022007021125
464591UK00021B/691